Elite • 219

D-Day Beach Assault Troops

GORDON L. ROTTMAN   **ILLUSTRATED BY PETER DENNIS**

Series editor Martin Windrow

Osprey Publishing
c/o Bloomsbury Publishing Plc
PO Box 883, Oxford, OX1 9PL, UK
Or
c/o Bloomsbury Publishing Inc.
1385 Broadway, 5th Floor, New York, NY 10018, USA
E-mail: info@ospreypublishing.com

www.ospreypublishing.com

OSPREY is a trademark of Osprey Publishing Ltd, a division of Bloomsbury Publishing Plc.

First published in Great Britain in 2017

A CIP catalogue record for this book is available from the British Library.

ISBN: PB: 978 1 47281 946 8
   ePub: 978 1 47281 947 5
   ePDF: 978 1 47281 948 2
   XML 978 1 47282 713 5

17 18 19 20 21 10 9 8 7 6 5 4 3 2 1

Editor Martin Windrow
Index by Alison Worthington
Typeset in Sabon and Myriad Pro

Page layouts by PDQ Digital Media Solutions, Bungay, UK
Printed in China through World Print Ltd.

Osprey Publishing is supporting the Woodland Trust, the UK's leading woodland conservation charity. Between 2014 and 2018 our donations will be spent on their Centenary Woods project in the UK.

www.ospreypublishing.com

ARTIST'S NOTE

Readers may care to note that the original paintings from which the color plates in this book were prepared are available for private sale. All reproduction copyright whatsoever is retained by the Publishers. All enquiries should be addressed to:

Peter Dennis, Fieldhead, The Park, Mansfield, Nottinghamshire NG18 2AT, UK

The Publishers regret that they can enter into no correspondence upon this matter.

Many of the photos in this book come from the huge collections of IWM (Imperial War Museums) which cover all aspects of conflict involving Britain and the Commonwealth since the start of the twentieth century. These rich resources are available online to search, browse and buy at www.iwm.org.uk/collections. In addition to Collections Online, you can visit the Visitor Rooms where you can explore over 8 million photographs, thousands of hours of moving images, the largest sound archive of its kind in the world, thousands of diaries and letters written by people in wartime, and a huge reference library. To make an appointment, call (020) 7416 5320, or e-mail mail@iwm.org.uk
Imperial War Museums www.iwm.org.uk

Abbreviations used in this text

AA	antiaircraft
AFV	armored fighting vehicle (tanks, tank destroyers, assault guns, halftracks, armored cars, scout cars)
Armd	Armored (US)/Armoured (Brit & Cdn)
Arty	Artillery
AT	antitank
ATC	Assault Training Center (US)
BAR	Browning automatic rifle (pronounced "B-A-R")
Brit	British
Cdn	Canadian
CTC	Combined Training Centre (Brit)
Engr	Engineer
FA	Field Artillery (US)
HE	high-explosive
HMG	heavy machine gun
HQ	headquarters
Inf	Infantry
LMG	light machine gun
MG	machine gun
MMG	medium machine gun
NCO	non-commissioned officer (corporal, sergeant)
OD	olive drab
pdr	pounder (Brit gun caliber designation)
PIAT	projector, infantry, anti-tank (Brit, pronounced "pee-at")
Ptn	pattern date (Brit)
RCN	Royal Canadian Navy
RM	Royal Marines (Brit)
RN	Royal Navy (Brit)
SMG	submachine gun
SP	self-propelled
USN	United States Navy
WP	white phosphorus (smoke compound)

Unit abbreviations

Bde	Brigade (Brit & Cdn regt-size formation)
Bn	Battalion
Bty	Battery (company-size artillery unit)
Co	Company
Det	Detachment
Div	Division
Grp	Group
Plt	Platoon
Regt	Regiment (also Brit/Cdn battalion-size armd & arty units)
Sqn	Squadron (Brit company-size armd unit)
Trp	Troop (Brit company-size Commando unit, or Brit/Cdn platoon-size tank unit)

Landing craft abbreviations

DUKW	2½-ton amphibious truck ("Duck")
LCA	landing craft, assault (Brit)
LCI	landing craft, infantry
LCM	landing craft, mechanized
LCT	landing craft, tank
LCVP	landing craft, vehicle & personnel (US)
LSI	landing ship, infantry (Brit)
LST	landing ship, tank

CONTENTS

INTRODUCTION   4

OVERVIEW OF "OVERLORD"   4
Selection of the objectives . The beaches . Beach obstacles . Exiting the beaches

PREPARATION OF ASSAULT TROOPS   10
No.1 Combined Training Centre, Inveraray . Assault Training Center, Woolacombe

US UNIFORMS & EQUIPMENT   13
Uniforms . Insignia . Weapons . Combat equipment . Assault jackets

BRITISH & CANADIAN UNIFORMS & EQUIPMENT   22
Uniforms . Insignia . Weapons . Combat equipment . Battle jerkins

ASSAULT UNITS   29
The US infantry regiment . US Army Rangers . US infantry boat teams
The British & Canadian infantry brigade . British Commandos . British
& Canadian infantry boat teams

D-DAY   37
The run-in . Overview of the landings . Utah . Omaha . Gold . Juno . Sword

COST & AFTERMATH   61

SELECT BIBLIOGRAPHY   62

INDEX   64

D-DAY BEACH ASSAULT TROOPS

This GI bound for Normandy carries a typical load. His M1 helmet is covered with a small-mesh "stretchy" net. Below the M1926 life belt, the M1905 bayonet for his slung M1 Garand rifle is hooked to his M1923 cartridge belt in an M3 scabbard, and an M3 or M4 gasmask in an M6 case is slung to hang at his left hip. Two 48-rd M1 bandoleers give him a total of 176 rifle rounds, and two Mk II fragmentation grenades hang from his neck on strings. Under his left arm is a sandbag holding three 60mm mortar-round packing tubes. (US National Archives/NARA)

INTRODUCTION

Something between 130,000 and 156,000 Allied troops, including about 23,400 Airborne, landed in Normandy, France on June 6, 1944 – Operation "Overlord," known ever since simply as "D-Day."[1] The subject of this book is the first waves of US, British, and Canadian assault infantry and their attachments, who went ashore under fire on the first tide from H-Hour, June 6. (It does not discuss the parallel operations by the Airborne troops; these, plus detailed maps and much fuller accounts of all the landings and their aftermath, will be found in the Osprey Campaign series titles listed on the inside back cover of this book.)

This text focuses upon the assault infantry's uniforms, individual equipment including specialist items, and weapons. It also describes aspects of their training; their task-organization of small units for the landings; and their landing techniques. The available space naturally limits the scope of this book greatly, but it must be emphasized that while the core of the assault troops were infantrymen, all branches were represented, including tank, artillery, antiaircraft, engineer, signal, medical, reconnaissance, and other troops. Apart from attached specialist personnel, advance parties from many types of support and service units scheduled to land later accompanied the first waves ashore.

OVERVIEW OF "OVERLORD"

The selection in 1943 of Normandy as the eventual battlefield for the opening of the "Second Front," from five possible alternatives, was due to a number of considerations. These included distance from Germany and from enemy reinforcements; the range of fighter aircraft based in England; the sea distance from England; and the availability of a major port, to be seized from inland and reopened (the disaster at Dieppe in 1942 had ruled out a direct attack on a harbor).

1 Reference sources are still in conflict over the total numbers of troops landed on D-Day. On each beach so many attachments, and small advance elements detailed from later-arriving units, came ashore with the assault waves, and there were so many cross-attachments between units, that accurate counts are simply impossible to determine.

The beaches needed to be wide and flat, with shallow gradients to allow units and supplies to get ashore, so the many stretches of cliff-bound coast were obviously eliminated. Multiple exits from the beaches were needed to allow units to make their way inland, connect to the local road network, and rapidly expand the beachhead. The extent of German defenses and obstacles was naturally considered, but the reality was that all the potential beaches were protected and defended.

The obvious choice of the Pas de Calais, across the narrow 25-mile Dover Strait (which the Germans assessed as the most likely target) was rejected. The objective's distance from England was not critical other than in terms of fighter range; in fact, Normandy was the most distant of the possibilities considered. The Cotentin Peninsula protected the Bay of the Seine from the Channel's westerly swells, and offered the major port of Cherbourg (though this was fully 26 miles' straight-line distance from the westernmost Utah Beach). Another disadvantage was that the terrain behind the beaches would prove advantageous to the defenders, being an extremely compartmented labyrinth of *bocage* country, with inland towns providing the enemy with strongpoints on the main roads leading deeper into France.

The mornings of June 5, 6, and 7, 1944 were the only dates on which low tide was about an hour before dawn. There was also a full moon on these nights to aid the airborne and naval operations. The English Channel tide rises from west to east, so high water at Utah Beach in the west was some 40 minutes earlier than at Sword Beach 40 miles to the east. For this reason the landings were staggered rather than simultaneous. The Allies used the British daylight-saving "double summer time," so dawn in early June was at 05:15hrs with sunrise at 05:58 hours. Sunset was late, at 22:07, providing some 17 hours of daylight. Low water was at 05:00hrs, followed by high water from 09:54 to 12:45 hours. The scheduled landing time (H-Hour) was 06:30hrs on the western Utah and Omaha beaches (a half-hour after sunrise), and 07:25–07:45 on the more easterly Gold, Juno, and Sword. Americans expect June temperatures to be hot, but Normandy is on the same latitude as Newfoundland, resulting in mild day temperatures but chilly nights. An approaching storm front would bring rain on June 7.

The beaches

The beaches were technically called "assault areas," e.g., Utah Area, though the common usage is Utah Beach. Each area was subdivided into "assault sectors" identified by phonetic letters, which in turn were divided into two or three color-coded "landing beaches" – e.g., from west to east, Fox Green and Fox Red. If there were three beaches in an assault sector, White would be inserted between Red and Green. Area, sector, and beach widths

This pre-invasion photo shows the eastern flank of Omaha, looking westward; the Fox sector is in the foreground with the Easy beaches beyond, and the E-1 exit to St Laurent-sur-Mer showing pale in the center; in the distance beyond this is the Dog sector. Taken at low water, it shows the wide expanse of flat sand that the troops would have to cross while completely exposed to artillery, mortar, and machine-gun fire. The density of the various obstacles – largely submerged at high water – can be made out, and in the right foreground a rocky reef is incorporated into the obstacle plan. (Tom Laemlein/ Armor Plate Press)

Assault areas, sectors, and beaches

Areas, sectors, and beaches are listed below from west to east (left to right if viewing a map). Only the beaches actually assaulted have color codes.

Area: Utah

Sectors: Tare, Uncle, Victor, William

Beaches: Tare Green, Uncle Red

Area: Omaha

Sectors: Able, Baker, Charlie, Dog, Easy, Fox

Beaches: Dog Green, Dog White, Dog Red, Easy Green, Easy Red, Fox Green, Fox Red

Area: Gold

Sectors: How, Item, Jig, King

Beaches: Jig Green, Jig Red, King Green, King Red

Area: Juno

Sectors: Love, Mike, Nan

Beaches: Mike Green, Mike Red, Nan Green, Nan White, Nan Red

Area: Sword

Sectors: Oboe, Peter, Queen, Roger

Beaches: Queen White, Queen Red

varied greatly. The total span encompassed by the five assault areas was 62 miles, but only a small percentage of this was physically assaulted. Omaha was 11 miles east of Utah, separated from it by the Vire and Aure estuary. About 9 miles further east from Omaha, Gold and Juno were adjacent, but Sword was about 3 miles east of Juno.

While each of the selected beaches had its particular character, all shared some similarities, notably their very shallow gradient. The low-water line averaged 500–600yds offshore, but could extend further out. Some sandbars emerged above the low-water line, and between the low- and high-water lines were scattered numerous 2–6ft-deep potholes and runnels washed out by tides. Beaches were of compacted wet sand that could support vehicles. In many areas the high-water line was covered by banks of shingle – gravel, ranging from pebbles up to water-smoothed fist-size rocks – and lesser bands could form at the low-water line. It was difficult for foot troops or AFVs to gain purchase on a shingle surface.

There were also erosion-controlling groins (in the British term, breakwaters), low barriers of stone or timbers and planks running perpendicular from the dune line down the beach and into the water. Landing craft naturally sought to avoid these, as well as areas containing reefs.

US ASSAULT INFANTRY (1)

1 & 2: Riflemen, 116th Infantry Regiment, 29th Infantry Division; Omaha Beach/Dog sectors

The amphibious operation required the issue of life belts and the waterproofing of weapons and other sensitive equipment; extra attention was also given to the possibility of the Germans using chemical weapons (note A1's gas-detection brassard on his right arm). These soldiers wear M1 steel helmets with the 29th Div sign stenciled on the front, just visible under the camouflage net. The "M1941" Parsons field jacket, bearing the same insignia on the left shoulder, is worn over the M1943 herringbone twill fatigue uniform, impregnated for the Normandy operation with an anti-gas compound. The basic web equipment of an M1923 cartridge belt holding ten clips for the M1 Garand rifle was augmented with at least one M1 bandoleer carrying another six clips; the belt also supports an M1910 1-quart canteen and cover at rear left and an M1942 first aid pouch at front right. The M1928 haversack has a blanket roll tied on, and an M1910 entrenching tool and M1 bayonet in M7 scabbard attached. Finally, these soldiers both have the M5 assault gasmask, and the M1926 inflatable life belt. Their Garands are protected for the landing with either a condom taped around the muzzle, or a Pliofilm bag; the rifle was inserted into this butt first, and the end folded over and tied or taped – if necessary the weapon could be fired while still bagged.

3: M5-11-7 assault gasmask with its M7 case. It was usually strapped on the chest with the opening edge upwards, but some photos show it attached sideways, or even to one leg. The watertight M7 case was credited with saving some men from drowning, since it offered some buoyancy.

4: The widely carried general purpose ammunition carrying bag held most types of munitions used by infantrymen: 12–16x hand or rifle grenades, 4x 48-rd rifle bandoleers, 10x BAR magazines (carried by assistant gunners), a 250-rd MG belt, 3x 60mm mortar rounds, pyrotechnics, etc.

5: The disposable M1 ammunition bandoleer for 48 rounds of rifle ammunition, with one of the 8-rd clips that was loaded into the Garand *en bloc*.

Riflemen carried an assortment of hand grenades, including:

6: Mk IIA1 fragmentation;

7: Mk IIIA2 "concussion" or demolition; and

8: M15 white phosphorus (WP) smoke.

9: The cartoned K-ration meal (issued three per day) was often carried in the trouser cargo pockets; this is a pre-1943 carton in plain buff card, still in use in 1944 alongside the later pattern with brown, dark blue, and green color-coding for breakfast, dinner, and supper meals, respectively.

10: Most men carried several D-ration chocolate bars.

11: The M1926 life belt was inflated by triggering two internal CO_2 cartridges, and could be topped up by mouth using the external tubes. The belt was fastened by a zinc hook-and-ring type buckle marked "U.S.N."

RATION TYPE K
BREAKFAST UNIT

U.S. ARMY FIELD RATION K

Cliffs, too, were obviously avoided in the planning – except, for operational reasons, at Pointe-du-Hoc between Utah and Omaha. However, in the event the sea currents and winds pulled landing craft eastward, contributing to many units being landed anything from hundreds to more than a thousand yards from their planned location.

Beach obstacles

The Germans incorporated natural rock ledges and inshore sandbars into their plans for beach obstacles (*Hinderniβreihe*). Beach obstacles were of great concern during the Allied planning, as they hindered and could damage or sink landing craft. A significant effort would be necessary to destroy some obstacles, with numerous assets dedicated to the task. While the obstacles were of standardized design their emplacement varied greatly. This depended on the assessed likelihood of a specific area being assaulted, the importance of possible inland objectives, the depth of the beach, and the extent of natural obstacles behind it. The lateral interval between obstacles and the perpendicular distance between belts also varied. Obstacles were seldom emplaced in straight lines at regular intervals other than for short distances. Four or five belts of a single type of obstacle followed winding and angular traces, making it difficult to locate them during high water. Occasionally obstacle types were mixed in a belt, but some areas, e.g. parts of Sword, had only a single belt of "C-elements" close to and paralleling the seawall.

The obstacles were placed to be submerged at high tide, since it was judged that the Allies would land at high water, hoping to float landing craft over the obstacles and get the troops ashore closer to cover behind the beach. Despite this expectation, the Germans had ranged MGs and mortars on obstacle belts and groups, and barbed wire was sometimes loosely strung between obstacles to entangle floundering troops. In the event, the Allies assaulted at low tide; this exposed the obstacles, although they remained a hindrance to subsequent waves arriving as the tide rose.

Obstacles generally began 600–900yds above the low-tide line, in belts 200–400yds deep ending perhaps 200–300yds below the high-tide line. (The photos seen of apparent assault troops immersed in water among obstacles actually show follow-on troops arriving as the tide rose.) Often the outer obstacles were "Belgian gates" (in German, *C-Elemente*), though these might also be found higher on the beach. Gate-like steel frameworks 8.2ft high by 9.8ft wide, backed by angled steel beams and a 10.7ft-long base, they had concrete rollers allowing the 1½-ton barriers to be moved into position, but wave action and settlement had generally buried the bases. They might be positioned in continuous "fences," but more often they were scattered in belts at irregular intervals.

Inland of these, wooden stakes (*Holzpfählen*), similar to the inland "Rommel's asparagus" anti-glider posts, were planted in belts 10–30ft apart. These 8–12ft posts of 8–12in diameter were slanted 60–80 degrees seaward, and a small minority were crowned with *Tellerminen* (TMi 35). They might be planted in 1–3 rows – the more rows, the wider the checkerboard intervals between posts. Inland again, what the Allies called "log ramps" and the Germans "stop beams" (*Hemmbalken*) were 20–30ft-long logs with the seaward end dug into the sand, and the landward end angled up at 20–30 degrees supported by props 6–8ft high. The intention was to damage or capsize a landing craft that struck the beam and rode up it at speed.

During the afternoon low tide on D-Day, a casualty from the first assault waves on Omaha lies by one of the "stop beams;" somebody has laid crossed rifles, an M1 and an M1903, at his feet, while in the background engineers prepare to demolish the beach obstacles (see Plate D). Note that the slanting beam is supported by a vertical post midway, since otherwise the weight of a landing craft might simply snap the lengthy unsupported log. After months of immersion many wooden obstacles had in fact been so weakened that they did break upon impact. (NARA)

Finally, the steel tetrahedron or "Czech hedgehog" (*Tschechenigel*) consisted of three 9ft steel girders crossing in the center so three ends were angled upward, to tear open a landing craft or halt a tank. Most had large concrete anchoring-feet; set on tide-washed sand, the lower ends would anyway gradually sink in up to the crossties. "Concrete hedgehogs" (*Beton Tetrahydra*) were 6ft tripods of reinforced concrete beams with the legs connected by base beams.

While the obstacle-studded beaches appeared formidable in aerial photos, they were mainly designed to halt landing craft, so once troops and tanks got ashore they presented little hindrance and even some cover from small-arms fire. In the event, not all that many would be destroyed by demolitions during the assault phase, and most by tank-dozers and bulldozers. As much of a hindrance late in the landings were submerged damaged and stalled vehicles, and the lines of damaged and broached landing craft crowded along the water's edge.

Exiting the beaches

Some portions of the beaches, especially where they fronted seaside villages, were topped by 6–10ft seawalls on the high-tide line. Of mortared brick or masonry over a soil berm, they usually sloped inland at 50–80 degrees (so they could be negotiated by AFVs), but some were of vertical reinforced concrete. In some areas sand had drifted against the seawalls, making them lower and easier for infantrymen to negotiate, and they provided inviting cover for pinned-down troops. In coastal villages the brick or masonry buildings on the seafront might have been torn down, but many remained, often reinforced, and occupied by well-armed defenders.

Whether a seawall was present or not, above the flat, wet beach sand was a band of dry dunes 2–10ft high and between 200 and 400yds deep. This might be sewn with anti-personnel and AT mines and barbed wire entanglements – often only a belt or two, but some with wide double-apron fences enclosing concertina wire. Trenches and other defensive positions were protected by more wire, and in some instances mounds were removed

The most dangerous of the many concrete defenses constructed by the Organisation Todt were those protecting guns emplaced to enfilade the lengths of the beaches; their massive overhead cover and walls facing to seaward were seldom seriously damaged by the air and naval bombardments. Late on D-Day, this AT-gun casemate provides the site for a beachmaster traffic control point. All vehicles exiting the beaches were checked for contents, manifest, full-capacity use, and confirmation that drivers knew where they were going. (Tom Laemlein/Armor Plate Press)

and low spots and gullies filled in to deny cover. All forms of obstacles and barriers blocked the ravines and roads exiting the beaches: massive concrete walls and blocks, "dragon's teeth," steel rail barriers, antitank ditches, barbed wire, mines, and even remote-controlled flamethrowers. Millions of mines were laid above the high-tide line along the Atlantic Wall, but many had deteriorated due to corrosion. The most troublesome were those found in small scattered minefields behind the beaches and protecting the approaches to towns and fortified clusters, but in many empty fields the Germans had placed mine-warning signs without laying any.

At Omaha, dominating rocky bluffs rose behind the dune belt, from 100ft to 170ft high and sloping at up to 45 degrees. These were cut by gullies, ledges, and outcroppings, in some places still patched with heavy brush. Allowing exit from the Omaha beaches were five partly wooded draws, designated from west to east D-1 (on Dog Green), D-3 (Dog Red), E-1 (Easy Red), E-3 (Easy Green), and F-1 (Fox Red). These were blocked with concrete walls, AT ditches, and mines, and were well defended by fire. Unimproved roads and trails led out of the draws, with only D-3 at Les Moulins offering a paved road. Behind the immediate coast a further obstacle was provided by low-lying areas which the Germans had flooded by manipulating the sluice systems on waterways. This prevented vehicles from traveling off-road, and slowed, though seldom barred, foot troops.

PREPARATION OF ASSAULT TROOPS

Since the invasion threat of 1940 the majority of British and Canadian combat units had been based in southeast and eastern England, and their staging areas remained there. When US troops began to arrive in July 1942 they were based largely in the west. During the Allied buildup for "Overlord," hundreds of bases, camps, depots, training areas, and other facilities were scattered across England. Troops resided in tent cities, Quonset and Nissen huts, or were even billeted in civilian homes. Massive parks, dumps and stockpiles of vehicles, supplies, munitions, and weapons were built up. Training exercises intensified and evolved into rehearsals. Vast amounts of intelligence on all aspects of the objectives and the enemy were assembled, and countless briefing documents were generated.

British and Canadian assault battalions and supporting units were trained at **No. 1 Combined Training Centre (CTC)** at Inveraray on Loch

Command, and assault forces

Overall command of the European Theater was exercised by Supreme Headquarters, Allied Expeditionary Forces (SHAEF) headed by Gen Dwight D. Eisenhower. On D-Day the Allied ground forces were under 21st Army Group and C-in-C Allied Ground Forces, Gen Bernard L. Montgomery. For the actual landings "21st" was derived from the Second British Army under LtGen Miles C. Dempsey, and First US Army under LtGen Omar N. Bradley (not, as later, from the Second British and First Canadian armies). Each of the four US and British corps assaulted with one or two reinforced divisions, though each would soon receive follow-on divisions.

Utah
VII US Corps
4th Inf Div (8th, 22nd, 12th Inf Regts)

Omaha
V US Corps
1st Inf Div (116th*, 16th, 115th*, 18th, 26th Inf Regts)
Provisional Ranger Group
29th Inf Div (175th Inf Regt)
(*detached from 29th Inf Div for assault landings)

Gold
XXX British Corps
Brit 50th Inf Div (231, 69, 56, 151 Inf Brigades)
Brit 8 Armd Bde
Brit 4 Special Service Bde (46 RM, 47 RM Commandos)

Juno
I British Corps
Canadian 3rd Inf Div (7, 8, 9 Inf Bdes)
Cdn 2 Armd Bde
Brit 48 RM Cdo* (*attached from 4 SS Bde)

Sword
I British Corps
Brit 3rd Inf Div (8, 185, 9 Inf Bdes)
Brit 27 Armd Bde
Brit 1 Special Service Bde (3, 4, 6, 41 RM*, 45 RM Cdos) (*attached from 4 SS Bde)

Fyne in western Scotland. Established in October 1940, this was one of the first of 45 training centers in Scotland and southern England to provide a wide range of amphibious assault and related training. Inveraray included an RN base providing landing craft, 20 practice beaches, and seven troop camps for 15,000 personnel. Brigade groups of three infantry battalions with attached armor, AT, artillery, engineers, RN beach commandos, and other support elements trained for three weeks, with increasingly larger-scale and challenging landing craft assaults, obstacle breaching, demolitions, fortifications assault, signals, and other tasks. The units worked up to a full brigade group landing on a 2-mile-long beach near Strathlachlan. This exercise included aircraft strafing beaches, smoke screens, and live-fire assaults with small arms, artillery, and mortar fire (resulting in occasional deaths and injuries). Among other units, some 130 infantry battalions trained at the CTC, including 29 Canadian and six US. Units also conducted their own assault training near their home bases, including day and night forced marches with full equipment, cliff climbing, swimming with full equipment, range marksmanship, more live-fire exercises, and mock assaults and landings. If landing craft were unavailable unloading drills were practiced with wooden mockups or simply white tape outlines.

In June 1943 the US Army established the **Assault Training Center (ATC)** at Woolacombe in north Devonshire, on the south coast of the broad Bristol Channel. Americans had already toured and undertaken training at No. 1 CTC, and the ATC offered much the same programs. Information, techniques, and lessons learned were exchanged between the two establishments, though there were naturally differences in organization, tactics, and equipment. Besides training regimental landing teams and specialist units, the ATC also developed and tested equipment and techniques. These included the means of firing artillery from landing craft during the run-in, breaching with demolitions, use of flamethrowers, development of the boat team concept, and waterproofing vehicles and equipment.

Almost 5,000 personnel, including demonstration troops from 157th Inf Regt, supported the ATC, along with naval elements operating landing craft based at Appledore and Instow. There were individual and small-unit training areas with mockup landing craft, examples of concrete fortifications and beach obstacles, demolition areas, small arms ranges, an artillery and

Infantrymen of 1st Bn, Canadian Scottish Regt (7 Inf Bde, 3rd Cdn Inf Div) during Exercise "Fabius," April 29–May 4, 1944. This view, looking into the bow of an LCA allocated to the Canadian landing ship *Queen Emma*, shows a platoon's sections lined up along the bench seats, with the lieutenant center front. British procedure allowed embarked men to unbuckle their belts and unbutton epaulets worn over equipment straps, and the outer sections to swing their legs round and sit facing inboard. On approaching the beach the officer would order them to refasten their equipment and resume positions, and bayonets might be fixed before the final order "Stand by to beach!" (Library & Archives Canada PA-167300, photo Lt Donald I. Grant)

mortar impact area and bombing range, a DUKW training area, and the 3,000yd-wide Woolacombe Sands regimental landing team beach with inland exercise areas. These included assault lanes, where small units debarked landing craft and worked their way inland, overcoming obstacles and fortifications using live fire and demolitions. Undertaking three to four weeks of instruction, units worked through platoon, company, battalion, and regimental exercises with their habitually attached units.

All regiments of the 4th, 28th, and 29th Inf Divs attended the ATC, along with the 16th Inf Regt of the 1st Inf Div (that veteran division's 18th and 26th Inf did not attend, as they were to be follow-on units). The 116th Inf from 29th Div was the first regiment to undertake the ATC in September 1943, and it attended again in March 1944 as there had been so many refinements since. Units completing the ATC then undertook divisional landing exercises at Slapton Sands on England's southwest coast.

US UNIFORMS & EQUIPMENT

Planning for the Normandy landings commenced far in advance, and was supported by a robust logistics system in an industrialized Britain with extensive manufacturing and transportation capabilities. Logistics planning was quite detailed at all levels, right down to the specifics of what each man should wear and carry. However, while guidelines were published and precise allocations of supplies and material specified, it must be emphasized that there were minor variations between units (and even individuals) in what uniform ensembles were actually worn on June 6, and exact details are still the subject of speculation and argument.

Most uniform components were olive drab, but this varied from dark green to dark brown depending on fabric density and specified shades. It was directed that the assault troops and follow-on units were to be issued uniforms impregnated with chemicals (chlorinated paraffin and zinc oxide) for defense against liquid or vapor "mustard" (blistering) agents. Many troops avoided impregnated clothing, and there was argument about its properties; it was said that treated garments had a heavy, oily feeling and a foul smell. Impregnation did make the item slightly heavier and warmer,

US troops training in the Slapton Sands area of the southwest English coast debark from LCVPs. Such calm seas during rehearsals could not prepare men for the choppy waves encountered on D-Day, and of course the degree of confusion and disorganization experienced in a strongly opposed landing could not be replicated.

American landing craft were painted light gray inside and out. The white hull markings identified the class of the parent ship (APA attack transport, "PA;" APD high-speed/destroyer transport, "PD;" AKA attack cargo ship, "KA;" or landing ship, tank, "LST"); its hull number; and the landing craft's number. Thus here, "PD29-4" identifies the fourth craft from the high-speed transport USS *Barry* (ADP-29). This class of ship carried only four LCVPs, so they were used for initial landing training of small units. (Tom Laemlein/ Armor Plate Press)

This staff sergeant rifle squad leader of Co A, 1st Bn, 175th Inf Regt, 29th Inf Div is typically uniformed, with the tan (or pale greenish) Parsons field jacket and OD wool shirt and trousers. The division's shoulder patch is dark blue and light gray, and his rank chevrons tan on dark navy blue. Just visible hanging from his left lapel to his pocket is the brass hooked chain for a "Thunderer" whistle. Many troops carried commercial hunting knives, and this NCO is posed sharpening a Marbles knife. Beside his Garand rifle, at bottom right, is a "general purpose" ammunition carrying bag (see Plate A5), here holding four rifle grenades in their black packing tubes. (NARA)

and gave a smell of Clorox, but it felt dry and "slick;" a fine white residue, like sweat salt stains, accumulated in fabric folds and seams. Impregnation was effective for only two weeks before clothing had to be re-treated, and troops would be glad to see the last of these "skunk suits" when re-equipped after several weeks' combat.

All personnel had a Parsons or "M1941" field jacket. This light tan jacket was conspicuous in green vegetation, and was sometimes turned inside out to reveal the darker OD wool lining. Some, mainly officers, alternatively obtained the warmer tanker's winter jacket, a zipped "wind-cheater" in light tan with knit OD wool cuffs, waistband, and low collar.

The troops were issued cotton herringbone twill (HBT) fatigue uniforms, the shirt/jacket and trousers with large pockets officially capable of holding a K-ration meal carton. These garments were designated "special" if they had an overlapping internal neck flap and a fly gusset in the trousers, to help prevent

B

US ASSAULT INFANTRY (2)
1: BAR man, 16th Inf Regt, 1st Inf Div; Omaha Beach/Easy or Fox sectors

This veteran of Tunisia and Sicily has removed the bipod from his M1918A2 Browning Automatic Rifle to save 2½lb weight. (A larger-sized Pliofilm bag, not illustrated, was available to waterproof the BAR during the landings.) Just visible on the front of his helmet is the 1st Div's stenciled red "1" within a broken black shield-shaped border, but he does not wear a shoulder patch on his HBT fatigue shirt. He has shed his field jacket and tucked it into his belt at the back. He wears the M1937 BAR ammunition belt holding up to 12 magazines, but usually only eight, the fifth and sixth pockets being used for spare parts and cleaning gear; the M1942 first aid pouch and M1910 canteen were hooked to the belt. It is supported by the suspender straps of his M1928 haversack (see Plate A1), which might have an M3 trench knife with M6 scabbard attached to the left side. Again, he has the M5 assault gasmask slung on his chest, and the M1926 life belt around his waist over his web gear; the 16th Infantry were issued two of these per man, one to be worn around the waist and one under the arms, but the other equipment carried often prevented the use of the second.

2: Rifle platoon leader, 16th Inf Regt, 1st Inf Div; Omaha Beach/Easy or Fox sectors

This second lieutenant has had time to discard his encumbering gasmask and life belt. He wears his field jacket, displaying the red-on-brownish OD "Big Red One" left sleeve patch, with a gas-detection brassard at the right shoulder; his other garments are an officer's "chocolate" shirt (OD Shade 51),

and wool trousers, web leggings, and field shoes like his men. Officers armed with the M1 carbine wore the web M1936 pistol belt and suspenders. The front and sides of the belt are rather crowded: he carries on his right hip, obscured here, a first aid pouch, and possibly a holstered M1911A1 pistol, and certainly has his canteen hooked behind his left hip. Visible are an M1938 lensatic compass in its case, and one of two carbine magazine pockets. He has an M1936 field or "musette" bag crammed full of his personal kit and slung to his right hip, and on his left the M1938 dispatch (map) case. There is no room on his belt for the russet leather M17 case of his M13 binoculars, which he has slung on his chest. Finally, just visible slung behind his shoulder is an SCR-536 radio; in June 1944 the US Army were alone in issuing a radio to platoon leaders.

(3) A carton of six motion-sickness pills (2½in long) was issued, sometimes with a silver-and-black wrapper.

(4 & 5) Troops received a French phrase book, and *A Pocket Guide to France*.

(6) The M16 orange smoke grenade was for marking friendly positions by day.

(7) M1938 lensatic compass and its case.

(8) 6x30 M13 binoculars.

(9) The SCR-536 "handie-talkie" radio (overall length 12⅝in) was switched on by removing the conical cover and extending the antenna. It was powered by a shorter BA-37 and a longer BA-38 battery, inserted through the hinge-open base.

(10) The M9 hand pyrotechnic projector (7⅝in long, 37mm bore) took aluminum flare cartridges, here the AN-M44A2 single yellow star round for identifying friendly positions at night.

Photographed at Pointe du Hoc, this soldier of the 2nd Ranger Inf Bn is reloading a 15-rd magazine for his M1 carbine; spare magazines were in short supply. He still wears the M5 assault gasmask on his chest, and note the horizontal diamond-shape "Ranger" shoulder patch in gold-yellow on dark blue. (Tom Laemlein/ Armor Plate Press)

blistering agents from entering. Cotton gloves, leggings, and cloth hoods were also impregnated, but these were seldom issued or carried. Some units wore only impregnated wool flannel shirts of "special" pattern and wool serge trousers, others the impregnated HBT fatigues with or without the wool uniform under it.

Most troops wore the dark OD-painted M1 steel helmet and liner covered with a camouflage net (small, medium, or large mesh, mostly British- or Canadian-made). Some wore knit OD wool M1941 caps designed to be worn under the helmet. The regulation uniform headgear was the OD wool overseas cap, a "sidecap" piped around the flap in arm-of-service color; officers had gold piping and wore their metal rank insignia on the left front. Low-top russet brown leather service shoes were worn with OD wool socks, sometimes impregnated, and M1938 leggings, also impregnated; while OD leggings were available, most troops still wore the tan shade. The shoes had dubbin (grease) worked into the leather for chemical protection and some degree of waterproofing.

Insignia

These were limited. Most men displayed the divisional patch on the left shoulder of field jackets, and mid-sleeve enlisted rank insignia, but not on the HBT fatigues (though chevrons might be inked on by individuals). Officers wore rank insignia on their shirt collars. An approximately 1in x 4in white bar was painted on the helmet's back to identify leaders: officers a vertical bar, NCOs horizontal, though in some units only the officers had them. Often the division insignia was stenciled on the helmet's front.

Weapons

Since the weapons carried by infantrymen largely determined the combat equipment they wore, it is logical to list the former before the latter. The weapons employed by the US assault troops on D-Day were standard issue; effective waterproofing was a necessity, but weapons had to be able to be employed immediately once ashore.

The standard rifle was the .30cal M1 Garand, a semi-automatic taking an 8-rd clip. A supplementary rifle was the .30cal M1903 or M1903A3 Springfield bolt-action weapon with a 5-rd magazine loaded from a stripper clip. These were issued to the "overstrength" troops who reinforced rifle companies; some units acquired M1s for their "overstrengths" by swapping with service units, which typically had 25 percent of their personnel armed with M1 or M1903 rifles and were otherwise armed with carbines. The standard sniper rifle was the M1903A4 with a 2.4x telescope.

The semi-automatic .30cal M1 carbine armed most weapons crewmen, service and support personnel, and officers. It had a 15-rd magazine, but used a smaller cartridge than the other weapons of the same caliber. Submachine guns included the .45cal Thompson, using 20-rd and 30-rd magazines; the M1928A1 was being replaced with the modernized and simplified M1/M1A1 at this date. The first .45cal M3 SMGs or "grease guns" with 30-rd magazines were issued in small numbers in time for Normandy, but in fact few SMGs of any type found their way to non-Airborne infantry rifle companies other than in Ranger battalions. The standard pistol was the Colt .45cal M1911A1 semi-automatic with a 7-rd magazine.

Hand grenades included the Mk IIA1 fragmentation, Mk IIIA2 demolition or "concussion," AN-M8 white smoke, AN-M14 thermite incendiary, M15 white phosphorus smoke, and M16 colored smoke (red, orange, yellow, green, violet, blue, or black). Rifle grenades were the M9A1 AT, M17 fragmentation, M19 WP smoke, and various colored smoke and flare signal rounds. The M7 and M8 muzzle-mounted grenade launchers were available for the M1 rifle and M1 carbine, respectively, but with an M7 attached the rifle could not be fired semi-automatic. A few units still had one M1903 rifle per squad fitted with an M1 grenade launcher. The 10in M1 bayonet was issued with the M1 and M1903 rifles; there was no carbine bayonet at this time. Men armed with pistols, SMGs, carbines, and BARs might receive a 6.7in M3 trench knife, and many troops had privately purchased hunting knives.

The .30cal M1918A2 Browning automatic rifle (BAR) provided rifle squads with a suppressive-fire automatic weapon. At company level, infantry had the air-cooled, tripod-mounted, belt-fed .30cal M1919A4 LMG; the 60mm M2 mortar; and the 2.36in M1A1 AT rocket launcher or "bazooka." At battalion level they were supported by the water-cooled .30cal M1917A1 HMG and the 81mm M1 mortar. At regimental level were the 57mm M1 AT gun, and the 105mm M3 short-barreled howitzer – both towed by 1½-ton cargo trucks, though some assault units had M3 halftracks as prime-movers[2]. Man-packed M1A1 flamethrowers were readily available, but there are no documented instances of their use in combat on D-Day.

Combat equipment

While dark OD web gear had been adopted in 1941, many still carried tan-colored or pea-green gear, or such earlier items mixed with OD. The equipment issued depended upon a man's weapon.

A rifle-armed infantryman's web gear consisted of an M1923 cartridge belt with 10x pockets each holding an 8-rd clip for the M1 Garand (or two 5-rd clips for the M1903); hooked to this belt were an M1910 canteen cover with 1qt canteen and nesting cup, and an M1942 first aid pouch. The M1928 haversack was linked to the belt by its suspender straps; attached to it were the M1 bayonet in an M7 scabbard, and a T-handle M1910 entrenching spade or other tool (very few troops had received the M1943 folding e-tool by D-Day). Tools were allocated per ten-man squad, leading to uneven distribution: per squad, 7x e-tools, 2x M1910 pick-mattocks, 1x M1910 axe, and 2x M1938 wire cutters. A basic bedroll tied around the haversack consisted of two wool blankets and an M1938 raincoat. The contents of the haversack and bedroll were supposed to include spare underwear and socks, washing kit, 3x K-ration meals, 3x D-ration bars, and the mess kit, though in practice most assault troops left the latter aboard their transport and kept only the spoon. Instead of the haversack, infantry officers were issued the M1936 field bag or "musette," which could either be slung by a shoulder strap or attached to M1936 suspenders and worn as an upper backpack.

---

2 For fuller details, see Elite 214 World War II Infantry Fire Support Tactics, which cover the US, British, German and Soviet armies.

Wartime sketch of a 29th Inf Div platoon commander outfitted for D-Day; this second lieutenant differs from our Plate B2 in a few details. He wears a part-inflated life belt under his suspenders; he has chemically "impregnited [sic] jump boots," with a parachutist's first aid packet taped to a sheath knife attached to his right lower leg; his canteen and map case hang on his right side, and wire-cutters at his left hip, behind the assault gasmask strapped to his left thigh. (Tom Laemlein/ Armor Plate Press)

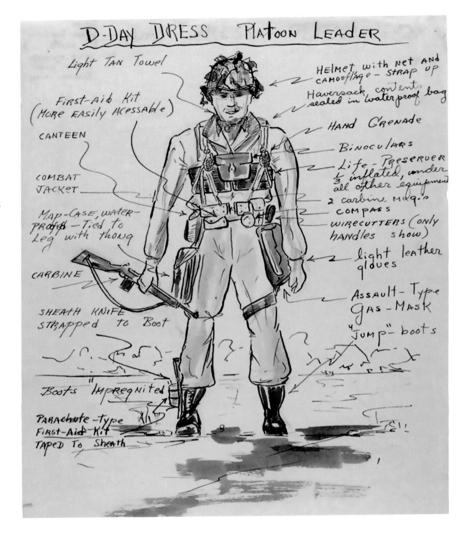

D-DAY DRESS PLATOON LEADER

Light Tan Towel

First-Aid Kit (MORE EASILY ACESSAble)

CANTEEN

COMBAT JACKET

MAP-CASE, WATER-PROOF — Tied to Leg with thong

CARBINE

SHEATH KNIFE STRAPPED TO Boot

Boots "IMPREGNITED"

PARACHUTE-Type FIRST-AID KIT TAPED TO SHEATH

HELMET, with NET AND CAMOUFLAGE — STRAP UP

Haversack content sealed in waterproof bag

HAND GRENADE

BINOCULARS

Life-PRESERVER ⅓ inflated, under all other equipment

2 carbine mag's

COMPASS

WIRECUTTERS (only handles show)

2 light leather gloves

Assault-Type GAS-MASK

"JUMP" boots

Soldiers armed with pistols, carbines, and submachine guns were issued M1936 pistol belts and suspenders. Those with pistols had an M1916 holster and a pocket for two 7-rd magazines; those with carbines, two to four pockets for two 15-rd magazines (five magazines were the normal issue); and those with SMGs, either a five-pocket carrier for 20-rd magazines or a three-pocket carrier for 30-rd magazines. BAR men used the M1937 BAR belt, with 6x pockets each holding two 20-rd magazines. Rifle-grenadiers used an ammunition carrying bag (miscalled an M1 ammunition bag) on a shoulder strap, holding up to 11 grenades.

Riflemen carried 80rds of ammunition in their belts, plus at least two (and sometimes up to six) 48-rd disposable cloth bandoleers. Carbine-armed men were often short of magazines, so additionally carried a 50-rd carton for reloading. Each man usually carried from two to six frag grenades, plus possibly a concussion and/or WP grenade. Leaders carried colored smoke grenades for position and target marking.

Company-grade officers had M1 carbines and field-grade officers pistols (though junior officers might also carry these). Officers had an M1936 pistol belt, suspenders, and musette bag regardless of branch, plus, for the infantry, an M1938 dispatch/ map case; M13 (6x30), M16 or M17 (both 7x50) binoculars; an M1938 lensatic compass, and a TL-122 flashlight.

For the assault troops, an M5 assault gasmask was issued in its watertight black rubberized M7 carrier, with the M5 protective ointment set, anti-dim agent, shoe impregnate, 2x plastic eyeshields, 2x gas-detection brassards, and a plastic anti-gas protective cover. Other troops used the M3 or M4 lightweight service gasmask in an M6 duck carrier.

Personal-use items issued for one week included: 7x packs cigarettes, 7x sticks gum, 7x boxes matches, a 2oz can of insecticide (louse) powder, 3x condoms, and 3x extra pairs of socks. For the assault, a waterproofing Pliofilm weapon bag, 3x ration-heating fuel tablets, a bottle of 100x water purification tablets, a packet of 6x motion sickness pills, 2x paper seasickness bags, a box of 8x sulfa tablets, 200 French "invasion francs," and a copy of Gen Eisenhower's orders of the day were issued.

Many assault troops were additionally provided a parachutist's first aid packet: this held a field dressing, tourniquet, morphine syrette, 8x sulfa tablets, and 5x sulfa powder envelopes. (Sulfa powder was no longer issued after June 1944, but was still in the hands of troops.) These were collected up within weeks, as untrained soldiers were over-injecting morphine.

Assault jackets

The idea of a load-carrying assault jacket seemed practical, given that the M1928 haversack was ill-suited for assault troops. With some differences in the pockets and other fittings, the American assault jacket (the official term, though it was in fact a vest) was basically copied from the British battle

Follow-on troops bide their time aboard an LCI(L) crossing the Channel. They wear HBT fatigue uniform, and their weapons are protected from damp in the clear Pliofilm covers issued to all the assault units. The foreground soldier has an 81mm mortar round tube tucked through the suspenders of his M1928 haversack. (NARA)

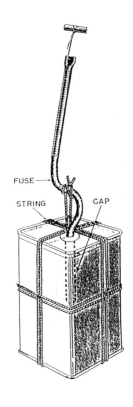

FUSE

STRING · CAP

Foxhole starter charge

To blast starter holes for hasty foxholes, assault troops were issued a ½lb TNT block measuring 2in x 2in x 3¼in, with an M1 fuse igniter (waterproofed with a condom) and 6in of safety fuse (approximately 15-second burn). Colored yellow with black and red markings, the blocks were carried taped to bayonet scabbards or pistol holsters, or inside the pack, with the fuse assembly carried in the canteen cover – it was unsafe to carry the charges fused. On Omaha Beach, fearing a German counterattack, troops inserted their blocks in empty cardboard K-ration cartons and filled them with beach shingle to make expedient grenades. Fortunately, no counterattacks occurred, but these charges were also used for throwing into German fighting positions and bunker embrasures.

As an ammo box tied to a Yukon packboard is handed down (right), assault troops jockey for position in an LCVP for the run to shore on D-Day; most are wearing assault jackets. Owing to their last-minute delivery from late May 1944 these had not been worn during exercises, and there was no guidance on what contents were to be carried or where; this led to rushed, inconsistent, and inefficient packing. While they accommodated a good load, they were an "all or nothing" item – a man had to keep, or discard, everything at once. A few photos show individuals still wearing them as late as August, but most troops discarded them within hours or a few days of landing. Not all assault troops were issued them, and they were unevenly distributed; some follow-on troops picked up discarded examples, but they too soon cast them aside. (Tom Laemlein/Armor Plate Press)

jerkin developed in 1942 by Col E. R. Rivers-Macpherson (see page 25). The latter was ordered in January 1943, and development of a US version began at the ATC at Woolacombe shortly thereafter. These jackets were made in

C US NAVY LANDING CRAFT CREWS

The naval task forces included some 2,600 landing craft. In the Western TF for the American beaches the sailors facing the greatest dangers alongside the assault troops were several thousand crewmen manning US Navy landing, control and fire support craft, plus Seabees, beach party personnel, and demolitions specialists. Included were US Coast Guardsmen under Navy command manning troop transports, LSTs, LCIs, and rescue boats. Those required to go ashore were generally armed with M1903 rifles or M1 carbines (see Plate D).

1: LCVP CREWMAN

The crew of a Landing Craft, Vehicle and Personnel or "Higgins boat" consisted of the coxswain (rear left side, immediately forward of engine compartment); a motorman, who operated the ramp winch controls (right of the coxswain) and manned one of the two 30cal M1919A4 MGs in rear "manholes," and a seaman manning the other; and sometimes a fourth sailor employed as a bowman. The basic seaman's uniform was a light blue chambray shirt, dark blue denim dungaree trousers, laced black leather N-1 shoes, and either a white sailor's cap, black knit watch cap, or the M1 steel helmet. Various types of jackets or parkas were available; this sailor wears the wind- and waterproof N-1 winter deck jacket, which had "U.S.NAVY" stenciled in white across the back of the shoulders (this jacket was also made in khaki). Partly visible under the jacket is a Mk 1 utility knife on his belt – see (7) and (8) below. The Delta Electronics Type JR-IS battle lantern was found aboard all naval craft; it used two 1.5-volt No.6 batteries. (For clarity we

have omitted from both figures the routinely worn life preserver – see 3 & 4.)

2: Landing craft control boat crewman

The steel helmet was often either painted gray, or displayed a 2in gray band, sometimes with a white or black stenciled "USN" on the front or back; being overpainted on an OD helmet made the band appear blue-gray. This LCC crewman wears a hooded pullover jacket and N-1 trousers both made of heavy wind- and waterproof treated OD fabric. He has a Mk 5 signal pistol, with its tan web holster and cartridge belt.

3: The general purpose Model No. 2 kapok-filled life preserver was issued to landing-craft crewmen in various shades of gray; front and back are illustrated.

4: Less used was the P6 single-tube Type B pneumatic life belt, much simplified from the two-tube M1926 and lacking its CO_2 inflation cartridges. As well as this tan fabric, they were also made in OD.

5: Most early-arriving Navy personnel carried the Army M5 assault gasmask, but others were issued this Navy diaphragm (ND) Mk IV type.

6: The Mk 5 pyrotechnic pistol (11in long) came with a web holster, and a 32-loop belt for its 10-gauge (.79cal/ 20mm) Mk 2 flare cartridges, which were available in red, green, and yellow.

7 & 8: Both the Mk 1 and Mk 2 utility knives were issued to landing-craft crewmen and other shore-combatant sailors. The Mk 1 had a 5in or 6in blade; the Mk 2, with a 7in blade, was a copy of the US Marine Corps'"Ka-Bar" Mk 2 fighting knife. Many sailors also carried jackknives in pockets or hung from belts.

the USA, and issued for the initial landings to some personnel of the assault regiments of the 4th, 1st, and 29th Inf Divs, and to officers and senior NCOs in the 2nd and 5th Ranger Inf Battalions.

Most jackets were OD in color, though a minority were tan. Laid out flat, they were roughly oval-shaped with two large armholes. On the chest were two capacious cargo pockets slanting inwards at the top, with flaps and quick-release tabs; two more were positioned below on the front skirts, and two smaller grenade pockets outside of these. The wide front opening was intended for ventilation and was fastened only by two release tabs; some men fastened only the lower one for more rapid removal – when water-soaked the tabs swelled, and were difficult to release. The assault gasmask case was normally strapped on the chest, but this seriously interfered with the rapid removal of the jacket, and may have led to some men drowning. On the shoulders were quick-release tabs to secure weapon slings. On the upper back was a large permanently attached backpack, with a flap secured by two quick-release tabs, and a left-side sleeve for attaching a bayonet; low on the pack were straps to secure an entrenching tool. On the back of the skirt, below three tombstone-shaped waist ventilation holes, was a smaller "butt pack" with a single-tab flap.

Assault jackets were unpopular, being hot, heavy, cumbersome, difficult to remove rapidly (e.g. when first aid was required), and poorly designed for compatibility with other equipment. Wearing the M1923 cartridge belt under the jacket made the latter too tight, as its waistband was directly over the belt and the front skirt pockets were too high; it also made it almost impossible to access ammunition. To wear a cartridge belt with attached equipment over the jacket effectively and comfortably, the skirt pockets had to be almost empty. It was extremely difficult to attach a canteen, first aid pouch, etc., to the jacket; four pairs of large metal eyelets were positioned around the waist, but these were too widely spaced for equipment double-hooks to fit correctly – manufacturers were unaware that they had to be precisely spaced. Many jackets were discarded when troops disembarked into deep water, and others were abandoned on the beach.

BRITISH & CANADIAN UNIFORMS & EQUIPMENT

British and Canadian infantry (and the small Free French Naval Commando contingent that landed on D-Day) wore essentially the same uniforms and

This deceptively peaceful scene shows infantry of one of the two Green Howards battalions of 69 Inf Bde advancing inland from the Gold/King beaches in mid-morning on June 6, reportedly on the road from Ver-sur-Mer to Crèpon, where 6th Bn would see hard fighting. They wear standard battledress with Mk II helmets and 37 Ptn web equipment, and under magnification can be seen to display full sleeve insignia (see Plate F3). In both the resting and the marching files the corporal section leader, armed with a Sten SMG, is followed by the section's Bren-gunner. (IWM B5277)

equipment throughout, though there were slight variations between British and Canadian items.

The 1938 Mk II steel helmet was still in use, painted dark khaki-green, but the new Mk III "tortoise" pattern was also widely issued in British and Canadian units bound for Normandy. Regimental flashes were sometimes, but rarely, painted on helmet sides. Camouflage nets were widely used, often with ragged strips of brown and green burlap "scrim" interwoven. The standard uniform headgear was the khaki general service cap – a loose, beret-like item with a deep headband – bearing a regimental badge in silver- or bronze-color metal or plastic. Many regiments had their own unique headgear, to include Scottish or Irish bonnets and true berets; e.g., some Commandos donned their prized dark green berets for the assault. Canadians wore the same variety of headgear.

British 1938 serge battledress uniforms were drab "khaki" (in British usage, a mustard-brown color much darker than American sand/tan khaki). Canadian 1939 battledress, while of essentially the same design, was of a greener shade. The British battledress (BD) consisted of a waist-length blouse with a waistband buckled at the right front, epaulets, patch pockets on the chest, and buttoning cuff bands. The trousers, supported by braces (suspenders) and buttoning to the blouse waistband, had a front cargo pocket on the left thigh and a smaller front pocket on the right hip for a field first dressing, and buttoned tabs gathered the ends of the legs. The main differences between the 1938 original, and the economy 1940 pattern that was usually seen in 1944, were the exposure of previously concealed buttons; removal of the previous pleats from the chest pockets; and removal of trouser belt loops and leg tabs. However, Canadian BD retained these features throughout the war.

A light wool collarless shirt was worn under the blouse, sometimes with the addition of a khaki wool V-necked pullover sweater. British shirts were khaki with a shallow paler neckband; they were of three-button pullover type opening only partway down the chest, while the greener Canadian shirt opened to full length. Both armies issued a large camouflage "veil" of brown and green soft cotton mesh, often used as a scarf to prevent chafing by the BD collar. For bad weather both armies issued a sleeveless, crotch-length, three-button, brown leather "trench jerkin" with wool lining. Both also issued low-top black leather ankle or "ammo" boots, with iron cleats at toe and heel and hobnailed leather soles, which were worn with shallow, two-strap web anklets. In Italy the Canadians had begun using a higher boot with an integral one-buckle strapped ankle flap instead of the anklets, and these were issued before D-Day to 3rd Cdn Inf Div personnel.

A French-Canadian private of Le Régiment de la Chaudière, aboard the HMCS *Prince David* off Juno Beach early on D-Day. His Mk III helmet is heavily camouflaged with "scrim." He wears full sleeve insignia (for details, see caption page 38). From his uniform outwards, he wears an uninflated life belt, 37 Ptn web equipment in battle order, his respirator (gasmask) slung on his chest, and a rifle clip bandoleer slung under his left arm, but carries his rolled anti-gas cape in case he needs it as a raincoat. Note the seldom-illustrated waterproof cover on his rifle. (L & A Canada PA-142848, photo PO Donovan J. Thorndick)

British Army Commandos of 4 Cdo, 1 Special Service Bde photographed in an LCI(S) heading for Sword/Queen Red. This unit wear badgeless green commando berets; their shoulder title, worn above the circular Combined Operations patch, is "4 COMMANDO" in red on black. Over their web equipment they carry heavily loaded rucksacks with tools and ropes attached. Note that one man (center left) retains the older SMLE No.1 Mk III fitted with a discharger-cup for grenades, since this was incompatible with the standard No. 4 Mk I rifle.

Together with Capt Kieffer's 180-odd French Naval Commandos attached to them from 10 Cdo, 4 Cdo's mission was to clear the strongpoints in Riva Bella and Ouistreham at the far eastern end of the British beaches. The brigade's 6 Cdo would then lead the way inland to link up with the Airborne troops who had seized the Orne crossings near Benouville. (IWM MH33547)

Insignia

Full insignia tended to be worn on both sleeves, but this was inconsistent between or even within units. At the shoulder seam was an arc-shaped regimental title (in white-on-red for infantry, black or red on dark green for Rifle units, and replaced with various tartan flashes for Scottish units). Below this was the division badge, with beneath it one to three small horizontal strips in arm-of-service color, indicating the brigade's seniority within the division; all the infantry battalions that landed on D-Day wore red strips. Above the elbow lance-corporals to sergeants wore one to three rank chevrons, staff sergeants with a crown in the bend, and warrant officers (sergeant-majors) wore one of two grades of crown badge on the forearms. Officers usually wore khaki berets instead of the GS cap, and displayed rank badges on the epaulets in the form of one to three "pips" (company officers), a crown (majors), or a crown and one to three pips (lieutenant-colonels to brigadiers). These were woven in buff on arm-of-service color backing.

Canadian units had individual and often larger regimental shoulder titles in a variety of colors, and if the wording did not include "CANADA" or "CANADIAN" then an additional straight "CANADA" title in buff on khaki was worn below it and above the formation patch. The patch of 3rd Cdn Inf Div which landed on D-Day was a rectangle in a light blueish "French gray." The Canadians did not use brigade strips, but their rank insignia followed British practice.

Weapons

The standard rifle was the bolt-action .303in Lee Enfield No. 4 Mk I, and snipers carried the No. 4 Mk I (T) with a 3.5x telescope. The 8in-long No. 4 spike bayonet was standard issue, but commandos additionally carried the 7in Fairbairn-Sykes "commando dagger." Infantry NCOs and some junior officers carried 9mm Sten Mk II or Mk III "machine carbines" using 32-rd magazines, but commando units retained Thompson SMGs with 20-rd magazines. The British used the .38in Enfield No. 2 Mk 1 revolver or the US-made Smith & Wesson; by 1944 the Canadians, like the commandos, usually had the superior Browning 9mm No. 2 Mk 1 pistol with a 13-rd magazine.

Grenades included the No. 36M Mk 1 fragmentation (hand and rifle-discharger), the Bakelite No. 69 Mk 1 offensive (concussion), the No. 77 Mk 1 WP smoke, and No. 83 Mk 1 emission signal smoke (green, blue, yellow, and red). Additional hand-placed or thrown munitions available were the No. 75 Mk 2 Hawkins AT grenade/mine, and No. 82 Mk 1 AT "Gammon bomb." Rifle grenades were launched from the old No. 1 Mk III SMLE rifle with the No.1 Mk I cup-type discharger.

The .303in Bren Mk II was the section (squad) automatic weapon, a bipod-mounted LMG using a 30-rd magazine. Each platoon had a 2in mortar, the late models having a small gutter-shape base plate and being aimed by eye; in practice it was used for launching smoke and illumination rounds more often than HE. The company AT weapon, usually dispersed to the platoons, was the projector, infantry, anti-tank Mk I (PIAT), launching a 3.5in rocket.

The battalion-level support company had both 3in Mk II mortars and 6-pdr Mk IV AT guns. A platoon of .303in water-cooled Vickers Mk I MMGs from the divisional MG battalion was routinely attached to each infantry battalion. These support weapons were transported in (or in the case of the 6-pdr, towed by) full-tracked Universal (aka "Bren gun") carriers.

Combat equipment

Most 37 Pattern web equipment was made in a drab tan-khaki color, but a greenish powder ("blanco") was issued, which was mixed with water and brushed on to give a matt finish in No.3 Khaki Green. The degree to which this was done varied widely, but after it had been "blancoed" webbing retained a greenish shade, so the exact colors of equipment worn in the field differed considerably.

A rifleman wore a waist belt and braces (suspenders), supporting a pair of large "basic" pouches for a range of munitions; a 1qt Mk VI water bottle in a strapping or sleeve carrier; the bayonet scabbard in a web frog (carrier); and at the back the horizontal carrier for an entrenching tool – a small combination pick-mattock with detachable handle. Battle order as worn by the first assault waves included the haversack ("small pack"), with L-shape supporting straps that fitted over the belt suspenders and hooked to the basic pouches, thus allowing the pack to be dropped while retaining the belt kit. The haversack, with a two-strap flap, accommodated (officially) a second water bottle, nesting mess tins with at least one 24-hour ration pack, an emergency ration (tear-open brass tin with enriched chocolate bars), and the enameled mug (usually hung outside on a flap strap); the "cardigan" sweater, spare socks, towel, and a roll-up "holdall" with cutlery, shaving and cleaning items, and a "housewife" sewing and darning kit. The rubberized canvas groundsheet (rain cape) was carried folded under the haversack flap, and the anti-gas cape (actually a sleeved coat, of treated cotton) was usually rolled and tied with tape on top of it. The Mk II light respirator (gasmask) was carried slung separately on the chest or hip in a green canvas case, which also held 6x cellophane anti-gas eyeshields, 2x tins of anti-gas ointment, a tin of anti-fogging cloths, and a gas-detection brassard.

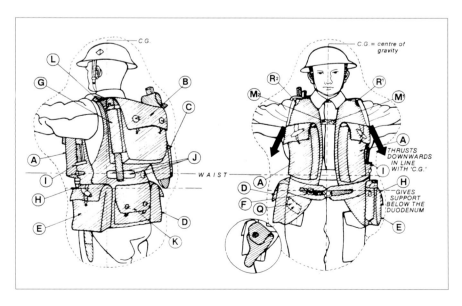

Diagram from the instruction manual issued with the British battle jerkin. **(A)** Chest pockets, shaped for Bren mags but just as versatile as the 37 Ptn basic pouches. **(D & E)** Skirt side pockets, for a water bottle and more munitions; **(H)** sleeve for bayonet scabbard, and **(Q)** strap for pistol holster. **(B)** Upper rear pack, holding (officially) the anti-gas cape, mess tins, cutlery, mug, 2x 24-hour ration packs, emergency ration, groundsheet, blanket, and a second water bottle or more munitions. Sleeves on its left and right side surfaces **(G & C)** held the entrenching-tool handle or a skein of toggle rope, and a machete, respectively. Below three ventilation holes **(J)** around the rear waist, the lower pocket **(K)** hung loose on corner-straps, holding the entrenching-tool head; this was padded by "soft kit" carried in an interior pocket. (Private collection)

A ten-man section might also carry up to five general service (GS) shovels, two GS pickaxes, and a machete (carried by the corporal section commander or the LMG lance-corporal); these larger tools made digging-in much easier than with entrenching tools alone. Folding wirecutters were also liberally distributed. Commandos were routinely issued with – and some other troops acquired – a 1in diameter, 6.4ft-long "toggle rope" with a loop in one end and a wooden toggle making a T-shape at the other; as many ropes as desired could thus be linked together, and had many uses.

Full marching order was worn by most follow-on and reserve infantry on D-Day, to include the Commandos and Beach Groups. This featured the 08 Ptn "large pack" worn on the back with the haversack displaced to the left hip, but capacious rucksacks were worn instead by some commandos. Those not assigned to the initial assault waves were usually heavily burdened, particularly with extra ammunition for the crew-served weapons.

In one pouch a rifleman carried 50rds of ammunition, and one or two No. 36 grenades. While the No.4 rifle had a 10-rd detachable magazine this was only removed for cleaning; no spare magazines were carried, and loading was by "stripping" the rounds out of the 5-rd clips down into the magazine by thumb pressure. For D-Day most infantrymen additionally carried at least one disposable 50-rd five-pocket bandoleer. In his second pouch each rifleman also carried 2x 30-rd magazines for the section's Bren LMG, or 2x rounds for the platoon's 2in mortar. With one or two of them carrying four mags in extra pairs of "utility" pouches, the section's three-man

---

D **OBSTACLE CLEARANCE**

Among the non-infantry units well represented in the assault waves were the Navy Combat Demolition Units (NCDUs) trained at the Scout and Raider School in Florida. In England they were merged with Army engineers to form joint Gap Assault Teams, each with 14 Navy and 27 Army personnel, and – theoretically – support from a Sherman tank-dozer. After only two weeks for joint training, the teams crossed the Channel in LCMs, every half-dozen men landing with 500lb of explosives in an LCR(S) inflatable boat which was to be dragged up the beach as the tide rose. Under V Corps' Special Engineer Task Force, 21 Gap Teams were landed on Omaha Beach, and VII Corps landed 12 similar Beach Obstacle Demolition Parties on Utah. In the initial chaos the first teams on Omaha took heavy casualties and lost most of their inflatable boats, but they eventually managed to open five channels.

This less hectic scenario is set during the afternoon low tide, when survivors were continuing to clear obstacles for follow-on landings. Most required considerable amounts of explosive to destroy them; doing so endangered nearby friendly troops (engineers were supposed to pop M16 violet smoke grenades to warn them), and scattered debris that hampered vehicles. In the left foreground is a Navy demolitionist (1); his helmet is marked with a 2in Navy-gray band, and he wears a one-piece OD herringbone twill coverall and paratrooper boots. The Army engineer (2) has two-piece HBT fatigues worn with leggings and field shoes; both men have web pistol belts and suspenders, and are armed with M1 carbines. The Sherman tank-dozer (3) in the background is fitted with an MT-S deep-wading trunks on its rear deck.

A way was devised to cut and collapse the massive steel "Belgian gates" (4) by means of 16 Hagensen charges. The flexible Hagensen pack (5) was developed by Navy Lt(jg) Carl Hagensen of NCDU 30, using an M3 2¼lb block of C2 plastic explosive; for lack of sufficient canvas tubes, they were made up using a GI sock. A pebble was tied off in the toe with twine; 12in of instantaneous fuse ("detcord" or "primacord") protruded from the other end, which was tied with bailing wire, leaving a trailing end that could be looped around the pebble "button" to fasten the charge to an obstacle. Any number could be used together, with the detonating fuses tied into a "ring main" of detcord linking any number of obstacles for simultaneous destruction. Here the Navy demolitionist feeds out special red detcord for this purpose, from a 500ft reel with detachable handles.[3]

The Army engineer prepares to blow a stake topped with a *Tellermine 35* (6). Poorly waterproofed, these often failed to detonate after months in seawater. If this mine doesn't explode when the engineer sets off his two Hagensen packs, it will be destroyed with a ½lb TNT block; he carries demolition materials in an M2 ammunition bag slung over his torso front and back. Many of the posts anyway lacked mines, but might instead be tipped with an iron spike (7) to rip into a landing craft's wooden hull. In the distance, a DUKW 2½-ton amphibian truck blazes, probably hit by mortar fire (8); these "Ducks" were mostly used to bring in artillery ammunition, being prized for their ability to run it straight up the beach and on to where it was needed. In the foreground are a demolition satchel charge (9), and a Size 1 all-purpose waterproof bag (10).

3 For fuller details of demolitions, see Elite 144, *US World War II Amphibious Tactics, Mediterranean & European Theaters*; and Elite 203, *World War II US Navy Special Warfare Units*.

A view eastward from around the junction of Sword/Queen White and (background) Queen Red beaches, perhaps at about H+75/ 08:45hrs on D-Day, when the sector was still under heavy fire from the German strongpoint "Cod;" in the background are medics from 8 Inf Bde's 8th Field Ambulance. The foreground soldiers are sappers of 84th Field Coy RE, part of 5th Beach Group (note white-painted band of the Beach Groups visible under the nets and scrim on their Mk II helmets, and the right-hand man's just-visible anchor shoulder patch). Both wear battle jerkins, the right-hand man with his entrenching-tool handle and a machete visible on the sides of the upper backpack. Despite the jerkin's rational design, note the extra stowage that was still necessary: the anti-gas cape rolled on top of the backpack, the gasmask slung on the chest, a substantial bedroll carried low on the back, and other items. (IWM B5114)

Bren group carried at least 13 and sometimes 17 magazines, giving a total of 27–31 for the section counting those carried by the riflemen. The Bren No.1 also carried a slung "wallet" with accessories and spares, and the No.2 a web "holdall" with a spare barrel and maintenance kit.

Platoon officers and NCOs armed with Sten SMGs carried at least five 32-rd magazines. Revolver-armed men had a 12-rd cartridge pocket, and commandos a two-pocket magazine carrier for the 9mm Browning or US .45cal M1911A1 pistols. Officers' web belt and braces supported a pocket for a prismatic compass, the revolver cartridge pouch, a holster ("pistol case"), and binocular case. The haversack was replaced with a similar-sized "valise," worn on the back or left side, plus a map case; both officers and NCOs carried a flashlight ("electric lamp"). Officers who preferred to carry Stens or rifles consequently wore one or both basic pouches like their men.

Other items carried stuffed into the haversack might include a tin with 2x bottles of water purifying tablets; a collapsible 3-vane heating stand and tin of 6x solid fuel discs, or a privately acquired "Tommy cooker;" a tin of 50 cigarettes; tins of blanco and boot dubbin; a wool knit "cap, comforter;" plus – universally, in a trouser pocket – an issue jackknife with marlin spike, often secured to a cord around the waist. Shell dressings – larger than the field first dressing carried in the trouser pocket – were often taped to or slipped under the helmet's camouflage net.

The original **British battle jerkin** had significant differences from the US assault jacket. Made of stiffer dark brown canvas, it fastened across the open front with two buckled web straps, but all pockets and packs fastened simply with cord loops over loose wooden toggles. It had four large front and side pockets, and upper and lower backpacks (see accompanying diagram for details); the rear skirt had a cotton interior pocket marked for "soft kit;" and on each shoulder lengths of whipcord allowed random attachments. Only the gasmask had to be slung separately, although in practice the actual arrangement of items in and over the jerkin varied widely. A second, "skeleton" pattern harness was also seen on D-Day; this was basically a brown canvas "Y" with a waistband and two front fastenings, incorporating only the chest pouches and rear attachment straps for a water bottle carrier. British and Canadian assault units had large numbers of battle jerkins available on D-Day (see Plate F), but relatively few were used, and fewer were retained, for the same reasons as the American vest.

ASSAULT UNITS

Three infantry regiments or three infantry brigades were assigned to US or British/Canadian infantry divisions, respectively; both regiment and brigade comprised three infantry battalions. While the US regiment had some organic support units, D-Day assault regiments also received significant reinforcements. The British/Canadian brigade had no integral support units, relying on the division for supporting attachments. Such reinforcements included tank, antitank, antiaircraft, engineer, medical, and services units. For Normandy, additional units provided to regiments and brigades were mainly attached solely for the assault landing; once ashore, after accomplishing specific missions or at a designated time, they would revert to the control of other headquarters. It must be emphasized that no two assault regiments/brigades were task-organized exactly the same. Their internal organization was also adapted, down to platoon level, to accommodate landing craft capacity or specific missions ashore. US regiments with attachments were referred to as "regimental landing teams" and their component units as "battalion landing teams" (RCTs & BLTs), while enhanced British/Canadian infantry brigades were known as "brigade groups."

The US infantry regiment

The 3,257-man infantry regiment provided the basis for the four US regimental landing teams. Regimental units included the 107-man HQ and HQ company (HQ, communication, intelligence and reconnaissance platoons); 115-man service company (HQ, transportation platoons); 118-man cannon company (6x 105mm snub-nose howitzers); 165-man AT company (9x 57mm AT guns plus AT mine platoon); and 135-man medical detachment.

The three 871-man infantry battalions (1st–3rd) each had an HQ & HQ company (HQ section; communication, ammunition and pioneer, and AT – 3x 57mm – platoons); a heavy weapons company (Cos D, H, M); and three rifle companies (1st Bn, A–C; 2nd Bn, E–G; 3rd Bn, I, K, L – no Co J).

The 166-man heavy weapons company had three HMG platoons, each with 4x M1917A1 water-cooled HMG squads divided into 2x two-gun sections. Platoons and sections were attached to rifle companies, although some might remain under battalion control. The mortar platoon had 6x 81mm M1 mortar squads in 3x two-squad sections. During the landing the 81mm mortars were allocated to rifle companies, but normally they operated under centralized battalion control.

The rifle company had a strength of 193 men plus up to 40 "overstrength." The overstrength did not always accompany the assault companies, but came ashore later to reinforce them and as replacements. At normal strength a rifle company consisted of a 35-man HQ, including 17 basic privates serving as replacements (in addition to overstrengths or simply counted as overstrengths). The HQ included the CO (captain), XO (first lieutenant), first sergeant, communication sergeant, bugler, three messengers, seven cooks, supply sergeant, armorer, and clerk. The company's three 41-man rifle platoons had an HQ with the platoon leader, sergeant, a guide, and two

D-Day first & follow-up wave assault infantry units (as deployed, west to east)

Regiment/brigade	Parent division	Beach
US 8th Infantry Regiment:	4th US Infantry Division	Utah
(1/ & 2/BLTs)		
(3/ & 1/22nd Inf BLTs; 3/8th & 2/22nd BLTs)		
US 116th Inf Regt:	29th US Inf Div*	Omaha
(1/ & 2/BLTs)		
(3/BLT)		
US 16th Inf Regt:	1st US Inf Div	Omaha
(2/ & 3/BLTs)		
(1/BLT)		
Brit 231 Inf Brigade:	50th Brit Inf Div	Gold
(1st Bn Hampshire Regt, 1st Bn Dorsetshire Regt)		
(2nd Bn Devonshire Regt)		
Brit 69 Inf Bde:	50th Brit Inf Div	Gold
(6th Bn Green Howards, 5th Bn E. Yorkshire Regt)		
(7th Bn Green Howards)		
Cdn 7 Inf Bde:	3rd Cdn Inf Div	Juno
(R. Winnipeg Rifles Regt, Regina Rifle Regt**)		
(1st Bn Cdn Scottish Regt)		
Cdn 8 Inf Bde:	3rd Cdn Inf Div	Juno
(Queen's Own Rifles Regt, North Shore Regt**)		
(Régt de la Chaudière**)		
Brit 8 Inf Bde:	3rd Brit Inf Div	Sword
(1st Bn S. Lancashire Regt, 2nd Bn E. Yorkshire Regt)		
(1st Bn Suffolk Regt)		

Notes:

First two bracketed units of regt/bde = first wave; third etc bracketed unit, follow-up wave.

* = attached to 1st Infantry Division for the landing.

** = all Canadian "regiments" listed were single-battalion units.

messengers. The three 12-man rifle squads had a leader, assistant leader/grenadier, BAR-man, assistant BAR-man, BAR ammunition bearer, and seven riflemen, of whom two were designated as scouts, at least on paper. All platoon personnel were armed with M1 rifles except the BAR men, and the platoon leader with a carbine. The 35-man weapons platoon had a six-man HQ with the platoon leader and sergeant, two messengers, and (nominally) drivers for the two jeeps, though the latter were turned over to battalion control. The 12-man LMG section had a two-man HQ and 2x five-man, one-gun LMG squads; the 17-man mortar section had a two-man HQ and 3x five-man, one-tube 60mm mortar squads. Total rifle company weapons were 111x rifles, 33x carbines, 20x pistols, 9x BARs, 2x LMGs, 3x 60mm mortars and 8x bazookas. Five bazookas were in the company HQ and two in the weapons company HQ, to be allotted as necessary.

US Army Rangers

The 524-man 2nd and 5th Ranger Inf Bns were, like the British Commandos, light infantry amphibious raiders, and were similarly organized in small subunits. The battalion had an HQ company and six Ranger companies (A–F); there was no weapons company, the crew-served weapons being incorporated into the Ranger platoons. The HQ and HQ company had 104 men in the battalion and company HQs, a staff platoon, a communication platoon, and a 12-man medical detachment. The small Ranger companies each consisted of a four-man HQ and two 31-man Ranger platoons; these had a three-man platoon HQ, two 11-man assault sections with a BAR, and a six-man special weapons section with a 60mm mortar and a bazooka.

US infantry boat teams

A US rifle platoon numbered 41 men not counting "overstrengths," but an LCVP carried at most 36 tightly packed men. Additionally, numerous crew-served weapons, HQ personnel, specialists, and advance-party personnel from follow-on units had to accompany the first wave.

Consequently, a platoon could not be delivered nor initially fight as a cohesive unit. Weapons platoons and HQs could not be loaded in the same boat owing to the danger of their loss if a boat was sunk. Supporting weapons had to be allocated to rifle platoons so they were immediately available after landing. Each "boat team" or "boat section" needed to be able to cut through barbed wire, breach minefields, destroy obstacles, knock out bunkers, and provide covering and suppressive fire, and needed a command and control element. To accomplish this within the companies of Battalion Landing Teams, the three-squad rifle platoons augmented with weapons platoon elements were broken up into nine varied-size teams armed with specific weapons and equipment. Although some argued against the inevitable loss of company cohesion, this system, developed by the ATC, had been proven in the Pacific. Once boat teams had made their way up the beach and gained a foothold, they would reorganize into platoons with two rifle squads and a weapons squad (of attached weapons-platoon elements). Once relieved by reserve battalions, they would reorganize into their normal companies.

It required seven LCPVs to land a reinforced company of 214 men plus attachments – essentially assaulting with six 30-man "platoons" plus the command group. There were differences in composition between regiments, and changes within companies, but the following six boat arrangement was typical on D-Day (see Plate E).

The assault boat team leader was a company officer, positioned in the left side at the ramp to lead the team off. The assistant boat team leader was either a platoon sergeant, weapons platoon section leader, or squad leader, positioned in the left rear beside the coxswain. He ensured that everyone debarked and that no equipment was left behind. In the bow was a five-man rifle team with hand and rifle grenades for covering fire, plus a couple of bangalores. Next was the four-man wire-cutting team, with more bangalores and wire cutters. The four-man BAR team had two weapons; then came a four-man bazooka team with two rocket launchers, and with them a two-man flamethrower team. The last off the boat was the five-man demolition team, with satchel and pole charges.

The company support team boat had a leader and an assistant leader as in the assault boats. In addition to a six-man HMG team and an eight-man 81mm mortar team, these boats also carried rifle, wire-cutting, and demolition teams, enabling them to fight their way ashore and gain a toehold. Company command boats had 16–18 men, plus attachments who were only to be delivered for other missions and not to participate in the boat teams' missions. The company XO was in the command boat while the CO was in an assault boat.

Each boat team leader had an SCR-536 "handie-talkie" radio on the company command net, and the command boat also carried an SCR-

On June 1, troops of 2nd Ranger Inf Bn board British LCAs in Weymouth harbor to be ferried out to the landing ships – on which they would stay, in great discomfort, until June 6. The stowed canvas cover could be rolled over the LCA's troop compartment in particularly wet conditions, but it seldom was. The right-hand Ranger wears the assault jacket hanging open; the man next to him has his bagged rifle tied to a bangalore torpedo, and both attached to a stretched-out life belt to prevent their loss. (Tom Laemlein/ Armor Plate Press)

Follow-on troops debarking on D-Day from LCVPs "PA13-13" and "PA13-27" belonging to the assault transport USS *Joseph T. Dickman* (APA-13); in the background is an LST. This angle emphasizes the small size and shallow draft of the LCVP. The men wear gas-detection brassards on their left sleeves, and in this case their helmet nets are wide-mesh types made from vehicle camouflage netting. (Tom Laemlein/Armor Plate Press)

300 "walkie-talkie" radio on the battalion net. The short-range AM "536" could not net with other tactical radios; it could only talk to other platoon leaders and the company CO on a single pre-set frequency, and could not talk to ships, aircraft, artillery units, etc. The FM "300" backpacked radio could only talk to the battalion and other company COs, but artillery forward observers had the similar SCR-608 with frequencies overlapping with the infantry's "300."

The British & Canadian infantry brigade

The three-battalion brigade had no integral combat support assets, simply the brigade HQ and a defense and employment platoon. All fire

---

E US LCVP BOAT TEAM

The LCVP was built entirely of wood except for the steel bow ramp and 0.2in steel plates along the front three-quarters of the hull sides. It could carry 36 combat-equipped troops; a light artillery piece or AT gun; a loaded jeep plus 12 men; or 8,100lb of cargo. Loaded draft was 2ft 2in forward and 3ft aft, and top speed 12 knots.

Since a 41-man rifle platoon and its habitual attachments did not fit in an LCVP, Battalion Landing Teams were organized into boat teams – four assault boats per company, plus a fifth support boat with heavier crew-served weapons, and a sixth command boat. Exact organization varied between units, and even within the same battalion. Here an assault boat team is shown disembarking at near high tide and beginning to shake out as they run up the beach; they are not under direct fire, but mortar bombs have begun to fall among the fourth obstacle belt of steel tetrahedron "hedgehogs."

The boat team was a self-contained assault force capable of direct and indirect fire, breaching obstacles and knocking out bunkers. It typically consisted of: **(1)** lieutenant team leader; **(2)** a five-man rifle team, one sometimes with a muzzle-mounted grenade launcher, two also carrying bangalores for breaching barbed-wire obstacles; **(3)** a four-man wire-cutting team, with two more bangalores; **(4)** two two-man BAR teams; **(5)** a four-man 60mm mortar team – one with the tube and bipod, one with the baseplate, and all with ammunition bags; **(6)** a four-man bazooka team, with two bazookas; **(7)** a two-man flamethrower team; **(8)** a five-man demolition team, with seven 16lb pack/satchel charges and three 12lb pole charges; and **(9)** the NCO assistant team leader. In some companies one of the BARs and one bazooka were replaced with a four-man M1919A4 LMG team, giving the other BAR to the rifle team.

The company support boat team possessed some of the same elements – **(1, 2, 3, 8 & 9)** – and lacked others **(4, 5, 6 & 7)**. These were replaced with a six-man M1917A1 heavy machine gun team, and an eight-man 81mm mortar team.

Other follow-on infantry were delivered to the beaches in LCIs or LCT(6)s, as shown here. The tank landing craft could take a whole reinforced rifle company together with several jeeps. Designed to haul AFVs and trucks, the LCTs had inside accommodation and toilets for only the crew of 13 and eight passengers, so they were hardly more comfortable for the tightly crammed infantry than LCVPs. (Tom Laemlein/Armor Plate Press)

support was either organic to the battalions or provided by attached divisional elements. On D-Day each brigade was also allocated an 84-man Royal Navy Beach Commando for reception guidance, with a subunit for each battalion (see Plate G1). The British and Canadians used the "first reinforcements" concept, maintaining a "left out of battle" (LOB) pool of 160 fully trained members of each battalion, including seven officers, to replace early losses. By nightfall on D-Day these would be badly needed in the assault units.

The battalion's 96-man HQ company (HQ, signal, administrative platoons, attached medical aid post) had no combat support elements. The 191-man support company (S Co) had a mortar platoon (6x 3in); AT platoon (6x 6-pdr, 6x Loyd carriers); 21-man assault pioneer (combat engineer) platoon; and a carrier platoon (12x Universal carriers armed with 12x Brens and 3x PIATs – these would land with the reserves).

Unlike the US battalion with three rifle companies, the British and Canadian unit had four (A–D); each had a 14-man HQ and three 37-man rifle platoons. The company HQ included the CO (major), 2iC (captain), company sergeant-major, quartermaster sergeant, a corporal and nine privates for general duties, with a 2in mortar and 3x PIATs. Each rifle platoon HQ comprised the lieutenant platoon commander, his orderly (runner/messenger), platoon sergeant, and two-man 2in mortar crew, plus normally one of the company's 3x two-man PIAT crews attached. The 3x ten-man rifle sections were organized into a rifle group led by the corporal section commander with six riflemen, and a Bren group led by a lance-corporal with a "No. 1" (gunner) and "No. 2" (assistant). All were armed with rifles except the section commander with a Sten, and the Bren gunner. Total company weapons were 100x rifles, 4x Sten guns, 5x revolvers/pistols, 9x Bren guns, 4x 2in mortars, and 3x PIATs.

Machine-gun support was provided by the division's MG battalion, whose three Vickers MMG companies each had 3x four-gun platoons. A company was attached to each infantry brigade, and one of its platoons to each battalion. The MMG platoon had 2x two-gun sections, with two Universal carriers in the platoon HQ, one in each section HQ, and one for each gun, to give the platoon eight carriers. Additionally, the MG battalion possessed a mortar company with four platoons, each with 4x 4.2in Mk 3 heavy mortars, also transported in carriers. Typically a 4.2in mortar platoon was attached to each brigade, with the fourth reinforcing the main attack or in general support.

British Commandos

Seven "Commandos" of approximately 460 men – this term identifying both their role, and a small battalion-size unit – were employed in the landings, administratively divided between two brigades. The 1st Special Service Bde consisted of 3, 4 (with 4 & 8 French Trps from 10 Interallied Cdo attached), and 6 Army Commandos, and 45 Royal Marine Commando; 4th SS Bde had 41 RM, 46 RM, 47 RM, and 48 RM Commandos, though 41 and 48 would be cross-posted on D-Day (see "Command, and assault units", page 11). In December 1944 the designation would be changed to Commando Bde, to avoid the unpopular abbreviation "SS."

The Commando consisted of an HQ led by a lieutenant-colonel, five rifle troops, and a heavy weapons troop. The rifle and weapons troops in Army Commandos were designated A–F; in RM Cdos they bore, for traditional reasons based on shipboard turret identification, the letters A, B, X, Y, Z, and usually S for the weapons troop. Exact organization and strength of subunits and numbers and types of weapons varied, but all units had higher ratios of junior leaders than in the line infantry. The following has been recorded for 1944, when Army Cdos had 24 officers and 440 enlisted men, and RM Cdos 450 all ranks but with fewer lieutenants. Each Cdo had up to 60 bicycles (landed on D-Day), 22 jeeps, and 12 trucks (D+1).

The 89-man Cdo HQ had intelligence, transport, admin, and 20–30-man signal sections with dispatch riders, plus attached mechanics and medics. Each of the five roughly 60-man rifle troops had a six-man HQ led by a captain and two (Army, one) lieutenants with a sergeant-major, signaler, medic, and perhaps a PIAT. The troop comprised two 27-man assault sections (Army, led by lieutenants). Sections had two 11-man assault subsections led by sergeants, incorporating rifle and Bren groups led by corporals, plus a five-man support subsection with a 2in mortar and a sniper. In some units (e.g. 6 Cdo, 45 RM Cdo, and the French troops attached to 4 Cdo), Vickers

The advance inland through Hermanville village behind Sword/Queen White, secured by 09:00hrs on D-Day by 1st Bn South Lancashire Regt, 8 Inf Brigade. Of the soldiers visible here, only the two medics with bicycles (center) may be from a unit actually integral to the brigade; all the others are attachments solely for the landing phase. The Churchill AVRE, named "Bulldog" and mounting the formidable 12in Petard spigot mortar, is from 77 Asslt Sqn, 5 Asslt Regt RE, 79th Armd Division. The MPs (left) are from a provost company of 5th Beach Group (see Plate G2); and the Universal carriers – note their extended side armor – are from the 3rd Inf Div's machine-gun battalion, 2nd Bn Middlesex Regiment. Among the priority vehicles landed by LCTs were "contact detachments" with radio jeeps from the divisional reconnaissance regiment to reconnoiter, and divisional MG battalion detachments to defend, the beach exits. (IWM B5040)

K aircraft MGs converted for infantry use were also issued. Allocation of small arms varied; sergeants and corporals carried Thompson SMGs, but lieutenants and sergeant-majors are listed as having rifles.

When landing, each section was supposed to carry a total of 37x 3in mortar bombs to be delivered to the Commando's 39-strong heavy weapons troop, which had 14 jeeps. Commanded by a captain and two lieutenants, this had a six-man HQ, and one each 16–17-man 3in mortar and Vickers MMG sections (in Army Cdos, led by lieutenants), each with two weapons. Commandos were also photographed in Normandy carrying flamethrowers.

British & Canadian infantry boat teams

While the British platoon was smaller than its US equivalent, it still had to be reduced to form a boat team. For D-Day each company in the first British assault waves was allocated five LCAs carrying a total of 134 men (Canadian companies might have six LCAs). The organization of the first-wave assault boat teams might vary slightly between units, but typically three of the company's LCAs each carried a reduced rifle platoon – two of them with 33 men, and one with 30 plus two officers and two enlisted men attached from the Beach Group (infantry Beach Co commander and runner, and Assistant Beach Master and runner from an RN Beach Commando – see commentary Plate G). The company's other two craft each carried 10–14 men from the Co HQ, divided for safety, plus a five-man Assault Demolition Team (ADT) attached from a Royal Engineers field company, plus half-loads of stores (for examples, see Plate H). There were no platoon

RM commandos on Sword Beach: landed at perhaps H+45/08:15hrs at the western end of Sword/Queen White, some 300yds from their planned location, these crouching marines are A Troop, 41 RM Cdo from 4 Special Service Brigade. They wear Mk II helmets rather than green berets, and appear to carry 08 Ptn "large packs" rather than rucksacks or battle jerkins. They are awaiting orders to move west against strongpoint "Trout" and the chateau in Lion-sur-Mer; A Trp suffered 50 percent casualties that day, and the unit lost more than 100 out of 450 men, so it was unable to make the planned link-up with 48 RM Cdo from Juno. The standing officer at right is Lt T. M. P. Stevens, who was awarded the Military Cross for his conduct on June 6, and was promoted captain on D+1. (IWM 5090)

radios; company HQs had two No. 18 sets on the battalion net, and one "combined operations" No. 46 set which, depending on conditions, had an equal or far superior range.

The infantry sat astride three seats along the length of the craft; one section each sat left and right under the thin overhead armor, headed by their Bren teams, and one astride the center seat led by the platoon commander. The platoon sergeant brought up the rear, with the 2in mortar team and the attached PIAT team of the HQ group. When the ramp went down and the armored bow doors opened, the platoon commander (plus any attached assault pioneers) led the central section out first, followed by the other two and the rest of the HQ group, to deploy forward in loose files into a rough diamond formation.

D-DAY

The run-in

June 5, 1944 was originally designated as D-Day, but the weather forecast for the 5th was threatening, with Force 5 winds, moderate waves, and a low 500ft cloud ceiling. General Eisenhower postponed the operation for 24 hours at 04:15 on June 4, and early-departing ships were recalled. During the 24-hour postponement the troops had to bed down on board wherever they could, and meals were problematic; they were strictly prohibited from consuming their landing rations. Eventually the meteorologists forecast a window of opportunity for June 6, with Force 3 or 4 winds and the skies initially clear for 24 hours; clouds would move in later, but remain at a minimum of 3,000 feet. While deteriorating weather was expected on June 7, Gen Eisenhower decided to take the risk: at 04:15, June 5, he gave the command "Let's go!" for Tuesday, June 6.

In the transport areas at least 10 miles offshore the ships anchored in their lowering positions where the landing craft would be launched. US transports first lowered their LCVPs and the troops then descended scrambling-nets hung over the sides (davit-cable load limits prevented lowering craft with full troop loads). The burdened troops descended the nets with some difficulty; the sea was choppy, and some men mistimed their tricky jump into the rising and falling boats. Loaded boats cast off and formed into circles as the next craft to be loaded took position. Some British and Canadian landing ships lowered their LCAs fully loaded, which did lead to some accidents and delays, but others used nets, which were always employed for loading LCIs. Once all craft were assembled they continued to circle until the order was given to position themselves on the lines of departure under the guidance of landing craft control boats. When these lowered their red, shallow-tailed "Baker" signal flags, the landing craft increased speed and headed for shore.

There were inevitable delays owing to embarkation and assembly problems, sea conditions, and mistiming with the naval bombardment. Some troops were aboard the flat-bottomed,

Photographed aboard the Canadian landing ship HMCS *Prince David*, these are British Royal Marine "frogmen" (a postwar term) from the Royal Navy's Landing Craft Obstacle Clearance Units (LCOCUs) No. 7 or 8. Each 11-man team, carried in an LCA, were to locate by Asdic and then demolish submerged obstacles, and to mark wrecks and clear approach lanes to the Sword/Queen beaches. In practice this mission proved to be impossibly difficult, and they were later ordered to join sappers clearing obstacles above the tideline. On shipboard they wear helmets and life belts with their hooded black neoprene suits; for the operation they wore goggles, swim fins, and the RN's Davis submarine escape set with an orange-brown chest bladder.(L & A Canada PA-143822, photograph PO Donovan Thorndick)

A section from Le Régiment de la Chaudière, reserve battalion of 8 Cdn Inf Bde, standing in their LCA hanging on the davits alongside HMCS *Prince David* in the early morning light of June 6; they will land on Juno/Nan White from about 09:00 hours. Two men have donned their anti-gas capes as protection from spray, and note the commando-style toggle ropes carried at left and right. The right-hand man displays full sleeve insignia: the white title "LE/ REGIMENT/ DE LA/ CHAUDIERE" on a roughly arc-shaped purple patch with an inset red edge; "CANADA" in buff on a khaki strip; and the 3rd Div's "French-gray" rectangular patch. (L & A Canada PA-131498, photo PO Donovan J. Thorndick)

pitching, rolling boats for hours, suffering the nausea, headache, vertigo, and vomiting of seasickness. There were never enough seasickness bags issued, and even helmets were pressed into service; spilt vomit washed around the decks, and its stink increased the problem. Soldiers were issued packets of six motion-sickness tablets, with instructions to take one 30 minutes before and one at the time of embarking, and another thereafter at intervals of no less than four hours. They contained sodium amytal, a sedative and barbiturate which caused drowsiness if taken in excess. Some men rejected the tablets; most seasick troops, once debarked, were soon rid of the more debilitating symptoms, but some reported feeling groggy, disoriented, dehydrated, and weak for hours after landing.

The troops were soon soaked with spray and chilled. The sky and sea were gray, and the water temperature was around 55°F (13°C) – cold enough to cause rapid hypothermia. The swells were 2–6ft high, increasing through the morning. The more heavily loaded a boat, the lower it rode in the water. Assault boats were ordered to continue to shore and not assist sinking craft, so the unlucky troops in the boats which foundered could only hope to be picked up by one of the Coast Guard's 83ft rescue cutters.

US Coast Guardsmen from one of the 60 cutters of Rescue Flotilla One come to the aid of struggling survivors from a sunken landing craft. Rising waves and wind-driven spray began to swamp heavily laden boats during the run-in; bilge pumps struggled to keep pace, and if the engine stopped they failed altogether. Hand pumps sometimes could not cope, so troops had to bail with their helmets. Operating off all five beaches, the USCG flotilla was credited with saving more than 400 lives on D-Day. (NARA)

Life belts

All troops conducting amphibious operations donned "life belts" when the order to board landing craft was given, and discarded them once they were ashore. The belt was less cumbersome than a life-preserver vest, allowing freer use of the arms – but it was impossible to effectively wear it over web equipment or assault jackets.

The US life belt was supposed to be worn under the arms, on top of the web gear, but in practice it was more often worn around the waist. (Many photos show Allied troops wearing the life belt under their webbing; this made it useless, since it could not be effectively inflated when confined by the combat equipment.) On occasion, two were issued (e.g. to the 116th Inf) – one under the arms, and a second around the waist – especially if a particular soldier carried a heavier than normal load. Inflated belts made movement difficult inside a crowded landing craft, so they would not be inflated unless going into deep water. The major flaws were that the belt would not positively keep an unconscious man's head out of the water, and – most dangerously – if it was worn low then the weight of his helmet, combat equipment, and ammunition threw the wearer completely off balance, making him dangerously top-heavy. Even if worn under the arms it prevented an up-turned man righting himself; all in all, in most emergencies a heavily loaded soldier wearing a life belt ran a serious risk of drowning.

Life belts were sometimes fastened to heavy weapons and to loaded packboards, ammunition boxes, and other equipment to aid flotation. Attaching them to demolition munitions also made it easier to attach these to obstacles in the water.

The **US M1926 life preserver belt (dual type)** had two rubber tubes covered with OD canvas, its seams sealed with rubber cement; at the front, two Schrader valves with zinc housings and spring-loaded screw caps held the CO_2 inflation cartridges. These were manually activated: the instruction "Squeeze arrows together with a hard quick grip and release" was printed on the belt's end near the valves. There were also two rubber oral inflation tubes at the right rear, for topping up.

The **British life belt** was a simpler and cheaper design, being a single flattened tube of rubber-lined light canvas ranging in color from tan to light drab; Canadian-made belts were white or buff, and both typically showed smears of brown cement around the bonded seams. Inflation was solely by a single oral tube centered on the front. On the ends were web tie-tapes to be bow-knotted behind the wearer's back; later belts had galvanized plates on the ends to prevent the tie-tapes from separating.

OVERVIEW OF THE LANDINGS

Machine-gunners on landing craft seldom opened fire before, and certainly not after their troops debarked.

From 100yds out the US coxswains shouted the distance to shore at 25yd intervals, and finally, "Ramp going down – Now!" Most boats beached at the water's edge, but many ran foul of sandbars, German obstacles, and wreckage. The engineman dropped the ramp, and the boat team leader was the first off. Some teams experienced dry landings; others plunged into water more than head deep, or anything between those extremes. Men who fell into deep water tried to save their lives by discarding weapons and equipment, but significant numbers of those wounded or helplessly encumbered simply drowned.

Most boats did not receive fire until touching down, since the low tide put them at extreme range, but German machine guns and mortars then commenced concentrated barrages, and some troops had to bail out over the sides if MG fire sprayed in through the open ramp. The further up the beach the troops advanced, the greater the intensity and accuracy of enemy

F | **BRITISH & CANADIAN ASSAULT INFANTRY**
(Additional material by Martin Windrow)

1: Private, 2nd Battalion East Yorkshire Regiment, 8 Infantry Brigade, 3rd (British) Infantry Division; Sword Beach/Queen Red

The 2nd East Yorks wore on both sleeves their regimental title; the 3rd Div's patch of a red reversed triangle on a black triangle; the single infantry-red strip identifying the division's senior brigade; and – as seen in several photos – their regiment's small white-metal-on-black Yorkshire Rose flash. This mortar "No.1" of a platoon HQ group in either A or B Cos, the first ashore on Queen Red, has discarded his life belt. He is one of many in the assault units issued with the canvas battle jerkin, though this was usually dumped soon afterwards. Other British units definitely known to have used them on D-Day are 2nd Bn South Lancashire Regt, plus 84 Field Coy RE in 5th Beach Group, and on Gold Beach the 6th Green Howards, 50th Division. 47 RM Commando were completely equipped with jerkins, as were part of 48 RM Cdo and some men of most others, including 4 and 6 Cdos; photos show part of 45 RM Cdo also wearing the "skeleton" version.

Both the Mk II and this Mk III helmet are seen mixed in photos of 2nd East Yorks. The anti-gas cape is rolled and tied above the upper rear pack of the jerkin. The GS pick is attached by the jerkin's shoulder cords, its haft forced down through the armhole to emerge from the left-hand rear ventilation hole. His 2in mortar is a tight fit in the machete sleeve on the right rear of the jerkin, and his respirator case is slung low at the back. He carries his No.4 rifle plus a carrier with six mortar bombs, here illuminating rounds.

2: Corporal, Regina Rifle Regt, 7 Cdn Inf Bde, 3rd (Canadian) Inf Div; Juno Beach/Nan Green

The Mk III helmet worn by this section commander, armed with a Sten Mk III, bears his unit's crowned Maltese Cross badge painted in green outlined with red, as occasionally seen in the field. The Canadian 1939 battledress, of a more "bronze-green" shade than British khaki, displays a typically conspicuous regimental title ("REGINA RIFLE REGIMENT/ CANADA" in green on a scarlet patch), and below the 3rd Div's rectangular patch his rank chevrons are also in regimental colors. Canadian NCOs were ordered to wear a gas-detection brassard. The 1943 high, buckle-flap boots were particular to 3rd Div troops in Normandy. At least parts of all the 7 Cdn Bde assault units – Royal Winnipeg Rifles, Reginas and 1st Canadian Scottish – wore the British battle jerkin on D-Day. Strapped to the rear vents, below the slung respirator, is a bedroll of blankets inside the rubberized canvas groundsheet. Awkwardly attached overall is the life belt issued to British and Canadian assault units. (*Militaria Magazine* No. 364, November 2015)

3: Company Sergeant-Major Stanley Hollis, D Co, 6th Bn Green Howards, 69 Inf Bde, 50th (Brit) Inf Div; Crèpon , inland from Gold/King Red

The only man awarded the Victoria Cross for his actions on D-Day was a 32-year-old former Merchant Navy officer and Territorial Army volunteer who was already a much-wounded veteran of Dunkirk, North Africa, and Sicily. He wears battledress with his regiment's title and green lanyard, red-on-black "TT" divisional patch, red brigade strip, and WO2's crown rank badge on the forearms; his partly visible medal ribbons were the Eighth Army Africa Star, 1939–43 Star, and 1930 Territorial Efficiency Medal. Although some of 6th Green Howards wore the battle jerkin on D-Day, Hollis did not mention it, and he is shown in standard 37 Ptn webbing plus slung respirator and Sten gun.

Hollis first distinguished himself above King Red beach by taking two pillboxes in front of the Mont Fleury battery, single-handed with Sten and grenades. A fragment caused a bloody gash to his face (he had already burned his left hand badly on the Lewis gun that he fired from the LCA). After the death of Lt Patrick he commanded 16 Platoon in the clearing of Crèpon during the afternoon. Under heavy fire, he took up a PIAT and went forward together with two Bren gunners, but they were unable to silence the enemy. When his two companions became pinned down, Hollis then went forward again alone with a Bren gun, deliberately drawing fire and covering their withdrawal. Wounded (for the fifth time) on July 24, CSM Hollis VC was evacuated to the UK.

4: Sapper, Assault Demolition Team, 246 Field Company Royal Engineers; Sword Beach/Queen sector

One of a five-man ADT attached to one of the assault battalions of (British) 8 Bde, he displays the 3rd Div patch between the blue and red RE shoulder title and arm strip. The "flamethrower, portable, No.2" was not much used on D-Day; however, Hptm Gundlach, 716. Inf-Div, said that he surrendered his bunker near Ouistreham after attack by British flamethrowers. One per company HQ were also issued to Canadian infantry battalions (or at least those of 8 Cdn Bde) shortly before the landings; weighing 64lbs and inherently dangerous to the user, they were unpopular. The "ack pack" harness incorporated a metal bar support frame, a webbing waist belt and shoulder braces, and a basic pouch for accessories; a pistol holster could be attached on the left side. The "Lifebuoy" 4gal fuel tank enclosed a domed central tank of pressurized nitrogen propellant, with fuel and propellant lines to a two-grip projector, and a valve control at lower right. The 1944 No.2 model had electric battery ignition, with the capacity for ten one-second bursts out to 120ft range.

An ADT consisted of an NCO, two men carrying the halves of a 75lb "beehive" demolition charge on packboards, one carrying a 40lb charge, and one with a flamethrower; their task was not so much to destroy pillboxes as to kill the occupants. The remainder of this RE company was scheduled to land before the follow-up companies of the assault battalions, bringing the sappers attached to each battalion up to four ADTs plus three three-man Mine Clearance Teams (MCTs).

fire. Many AT guns, up to 8.8cm caliber, were positioned for enfilading fire along the length of the beaches to catch AFVs in their flanks, and their heavy concrete seaward defenses had stood up well against the naval bombardments. It was found that the Allied bomber drops had achieved next to nothing. Bombardiers had delayed releasing bombs for a few seconds in fear that they might hit approaching landing craft, and entirely missed the beaches, thus failing to crater the sands to provide the expected cover for landing infantry. They also missed the obstacles, the minefields, and the substantial German *Wiederstandsnester* (Wn, resistance nests) and smaller *Stützpunkt* (StP, support points) manned by garrisons ranging from squads to platoons.

On beaches swept by especially heavy fire, forward momentum slowed drastically and even stopped as men were cut down in their tracks or pinned to the sand. Others stalled as they tried to treat the many wounded or drag them to cover. As small-unit leaders were killed and wounded, control disintegrated and initiative was lost, until bold individuals took it upon themselves to encourage men forward. It was sometimes hours before units established radio contact with higher and adjacent units, and contact with naval, air, and follow-on artillery was spotty or nonexistent. Communications also failed between the infantry and tank and engineer units.

Although the impressive naval bombardment had generally raised confidence, before even setting foot in France the troops had been suffering from hunger, lack of sleep, and seasickness, and now they were soaking wet, cold, disoriented, and apprehensive. They saw leaders and comrades mowed down, had a limited view and awareness of what was happening around them, and might suffer from blast concussion. Landing boats were being riddled, and vehicles burst into flames and boiling columns of black smoke. Corpses, dismembered body parts, and lost equipment were scattered across the beaches. Looking seaward only increased the troops' confusion, with scores of boats arriving, departing, or wallowing stranded amid floating bodies, and the follow-up companies and armor were delayed or diverted by the jams of craft along the tideline. It had been planned to get tanks ashore early and right behind the obstacle-breaching parties – first, duplex-drive amphibious Shermans "swimming" under their own power, then "wading" tanks landed in the shallows by LCTs – but in many cases the armor was absent or delayed, robbing the infantry of badly needed support against the enemy strongpoints.

A major problem for some units was being landed in the wrong places owing to the 2.7-knot near-shore current and the northwest wind, which caused many craft to land further east than intended. Disoriented and unable to pinpoint their location, the demolition teams tasked with clearing gaps had often got separated; either no gaps were cleared, or the teams opened gaps only for the assault units to arrive elsewhere. At high tide there were also problems marking cleared lanes for later-arriving landing craft.

As troops reached the seawalls and other cover near the dune line they were somewhat protected, and momentum was lost in many sectors. Some boat teams had been decimated or wiped out; the survivors were scattered, with leaders often casualties or separated from their

British first-wave infantry taking cover near the junction of the Queen sectors of Sword Beach, with part of strongpoint Wn-20 "Cod," just east of La Brèche d'Hermanville, visible in the background. Logically, this should be the left-hand C Co of 1st Bn South Lancs Regt on Queen White, tasked to take "Cod" in conjunction with A & B Cos of 2nd Bn East Yorks Regt alongside them to their left on Queen Red.
The two assault battalions' casualties on D-Day were: 1st South Lancs, 107, including the CO and ten other officers; 2nd East Yorks, 206, including nine officers. (IWM B5091)

British troops wading ashore from a 103ft LCI (Small), with "brow" ramps each side of the bow. On D-Day most Commandos were landed by these LCIs, which had a capacity of 96 troops – three times that of the smaller LCA. This British craft is not to be confused with the larger 158ft-long American LCI(L), which could carry a full company of 188 troops. Numbers of British soldiers were drowned, not only in craft sunk by enemy fire or mined obstacles but also by being dropped in too deep water, or being run down by landing craft still under way as they waded in toward the chaotically crowded tideline. (IWM B5092)

men. The growing congestion on the beaches made it hard to locate gaps through which to advance, and long delays ensued as subsequent waves of troops came ashore, in or out of place, with just minutes between the waves.

Nevertheless, even in the worst sectors small groups – sometimes from different companies, or even different battalions – gradually assembled or were gathered by NCOs and officers. Aided by the surviving tanks and specialized assault AFVs, at the tops of all the beaches the infantry eventually secured exits and began working their way inland, in many instances using more infiltration tactics than coordinated frontal assaults.

UTAH

The responsibility of the 4th Inf Div, Utah was a broad, flat beach, with no dominating terrain other than grass-covered dunes extending inland 150–1,000 yards. Most of the dune line was edged with a 4–8ft masonry seawall partly fronted with barbed wire, and 1–3 barbed wire belts backed the dune line. Four elevated exit roads from the beach were barricaded and mined, and vehicles would be restricted to these routes by a 500–1,500yd zone of flooded ground inland. The assault was to have landed on sectors Tare Green and Uncle Red to seize Exit 3 near Les Dunes de Varreville; a significant strongpoint (Wn-10) was located there, and the beach obstacles were dense.

Most histories claim that a combination of current, wind, poor visibility, and loss of many of the control boats led to the first wave landing in the Victor sector up to 2,000yds to the east, astride Exit 2. While these were contributing factors, the actual cause was that the lead LCTs carrying DD tanks of 70th Tank Bn were delayed, and because of rough water continued closer to shore before launching the tanks about 1,500yds out. Rather than

Photographed during training, this M4 Sherman DD ("Donald Duck") amphibious tank is in the process of collapsing its canvas and metal tube flotation screen. Eight US, British, and Canadian tank battalions were partly equipped with DDs for the Normandy landings (usually only two companies of each, with the rest being waterproofed and fitted with air inlet and exhaust trunks, to be carried in by LCTs to wade the last few yards to the beach). DDs were launched from LCTs up to 3½ miles out to sea, but increasing wind, waves, and strong currents swamped some of them and pulled the others off course. This led commanding officers to abandon the plan and carry them much closer in before launching, with inevitable delays.

Only one of 70th Tank Bn's 28 DDs launched 1,500yds off Utah was lost, but at Omaha 27 of the 32 DDs launched by 741st Tank Bn about 3 miles out soon sank. In total, of 220 DD Shermans available on D-Day, 43 were lost while swimming ashore. (Tom Laemlein/Armor Plate Press)

the LCVPs passing among the "swimming" tanks and risking swamping them with their wake, they slowed and veered eastward (left). By then they were too close to shore to swerve back to their intended heading, so they landed about 500yds left of the planned beaches, mostly in the Victor sector. Subsequently the assistant division commander, BrigGen Theodore Roosevelt, Jr., redesignated the beaches they had landed on, astride Exit 2, as the "new" Uncle Red and Tare Green, which has created some confusion among historians. The actual location proved to be beneficial, as it had few obstacles and defenses. Both strongpoint Wn-3 to the east and the central Wn-5 were heavily battered by the bombardment, which commenced at H-40 minutes against the beach defenses and shifted to inland targets at H-Hour.

On Uncle Red, to the left, the first wave's 20 LCVPs carrying Cos F and E of 2nd Bn/8th Inf came ashore at 06:30. The DD tanks of Co B, 70th Tank Bn, were late, arriving at 06:40. The second wave of 16 LCVPs carrying Cos G and H, 3/8th Inf, and demolition teams to clear the near-water obstacles, landed at 06:35. The third wave, with four LCTs carrying wading gun and dozer tanks of Co D, 70th Tank Bn, arrived at 06:45. At 06:47 four LCMs and an LCVP with demolition men from 237th Engr Bn landed to clear obstacles further from the water.

On the right, on Tare Green beach, the first wave was Cos C and B, 1/8th Inf with DDs of Co A, 70th Tank Battalion. The second was Cos A and D, 1/8th Inf, with Army and Navy demolition teams, and the third wave brought wading gun and dozer tanks of Co C, 70th Tank Battalion. The fourth wave comprised Navy demolition teams and a demolition detachment of the 299th Engr Bn, with bulldozers.

Enemy fire was light and troop morale quickly rose, after expecting the worst and landing in knee- to waist-deep water. There was little of the expected confusion. Only one of 28 DD tanks launched was lost, but initially they had little to do. An engineer platoon was attached to each rifle company; the seawall was breached at several points, and roadblocks and other obstacles were destroyed. The units funneled inland through Exits 2, 3, and 4 as well as cross-country. With so many demolition assets ashore, even though sufficient gaps already existed most obstacles were cleared for the benefit of later-arriving units. By 10:00hrs four more battalions had landed including those of the 22nd Inf, to be followed later by the 12th Infantry. Before long they were linking up with paratroopers who had secured the inland ends of the beach exit causeways.

By nightfall on June 6, 4th Inf Div units had pushed 2–4 miles inland. The 22nd Inf secured the beachhead's eastern flank and the 12th Inf the northwest, almost reaching St Mère-Eglise, an important hub of the US Airborne operations; meanwhile the widely spread 8th Inf defended positions to the west and south. With over 23,250 troops ashore, the division had suffered only 197 casualties in reaching all its initial objectives.

OMAHA

The 1st Inf Div was assigned to assault this widest and most heavily defended beach, together with the 116th Inf attached (on May 17) from the 29th Inf Division. The "Big Red One" would lead the assault with its 16th Inf to the east, and the attached 116th Inf to the west. Once these were established ashore the remainder of the 1st Inf Div would land, along with the 29th Inf Div, to whose control the 116th would revert on D+1.

A beach party for ship-to-shore communications, with an SCR-284 radio as used by beachmasters for liaison and naval gunnery control. Powered by a tripod-mounted, hand-cranked GN-58A generator, it could be used in AM voice mode, or for longer ranges in Morse code. Behind the left-hand man encrypting a message is the canvas carrying case for antenna sections. The man at the right uses an SCR-536 "handie-talkie" radio for short-range communication between subunits. The immensely complex plans for mutual communications on D-Day inevitably broke down under pressure of events, leading to confusion which was often costly in lives. (Tom Laemlein/Armor Plate Press)

Hell on the beach: under the threatening bluffs behind Omaha, LCVPs debark their troops, hampered by wind-whipped waves and the speeding landing crafts' wake, and under intense fire. (Tom Laemlein/Armor Plate Press)

Omaha proved to be the most deadly beach, and a close-run thing, with a withdrawal even considered at one point. It had dense obstacles, a broad exposed beach, extensive fortifications (11 strongpoints) and artillery, and bluffs up to 170ft high running the length of the beach. The bluffs appeared to be gradually sloped with even terrain; in fact brush and high grass hid many gullies, folds, and outcroppings on slopes of up to 45 degrees. These irregularities provided some cover to attackers, but also channeled them into approaches that the Germans were covering. The aerial and naval bombardments missed most of the defenses.

The 7,000yd Omaha Area was centered on St Laurent-sur-Mer slightly inland; 3 miles to the west and threatening both Utah and Omaha with its battery was Pointe-du-Hoc, to be seized by the 2nd Ranger Battalion. The essential objectives were the five beach exits, small ravines or draws piercing the bluffs and designated approximately by the beach sectors, between (west to east) D-1 at Vierville and F-1 leading toward Cabourg inland. Only D-1 possessed an improved road, and D-3 a dirt road; the other exits were merely sloping folds in the bluff. A road ran along behind the beach from Exits D-1 to D-3. The high-tide line was an 8ft-high shingle bank topped by a low masonry seawall impassable to vehicles. At high tide it was 200–300yds from the water's edge to the seawall, and up to 200yds from there to the bluffs.

The 16th Inf would land on Easy Red and Fox Green with two battalion landing teams abreast, while the 116th Inf landed on Dog Green, Dog White, Dog Red, and Easy Green, also two battalions abreast. The 741st and 743rd Tank Bns were to precede the infantry ashore with DD and wading tanks. The Provisional Ranger Grp (2nd & 5th Ranger Bns) accompanied the 116th, less three 2nd Bn companies detached to take the clifftop battery at

Pointe-du-Hoc. The follow-on RCTs were the 18th, 115th, 175th, and 26th Inf; the 115th and 175th belonged to the 29th Inf Div, to whose command they would revert on D+1.

Naval gunfire opened up at 05:45 hours. Launched in rough water 3 miles from shore, the DDs of 741st Tank Bn lost 27 out of the 32 tanks, drowning 33 crewmen. The 743rd Tank Bn was therefore landed directly onto the beach, at 06:29; the first-wave assault troops and gapping teams landed two minutes later. Currents, wind, smoke, dust, and misread landmarks caused many craft to land to the east of their intended beaches. Only two 116th companies landed off-beach, one in the 16th Inf area, but all the 16th Inf companies were 1,000yds or more to the east, some completely out of the Omaha area.

The troops expected the beach to be cratered for cover, but it was a featureless expanse of sand. The fire was extremely heavy; some boat teams were wiped out or nearly so, and whole companies were pinned down. Most boats beached on sandbars, forcing troops to wade ashore. Scores of leaders at all echelons were cut down, and organization and control fell apart. Even when troops reached them, momentum froze at the seawall and the base of the bluffs. Nevertheless, elements of the 116th Infantry gained four footholds between points just to the west of D-3 and on the beach's eastern flank. Gradually other elements began to work their way up the bluffs at several places, for the most part ignoring the heavily defended draws.

Penetrations over the bluffs were accomplished by increasing numbers of troops from 09:00hrs, but observers aboard ships could see only stalled troops, countless bodies, and burning vehicles, and erratic communications increased uncertainty. Vehicles landed by the follow-on waves caused severe

An LCT(5) lands troops off Omaha, well short of the beach obstacles. Some Sherman tanks can be seen threading their way through obstacles toward the seawall and the bluffs. (NARA)

congestion at the exit draws, and at 08:30 the beachmaster ordered that no more should be landed. The 115th and 18th Inf aboard LCIs were late landing owing to the lack of marked lanes through the now-submerged obstacles, which damaged almost 30 landing craft. The 115th Inf was scheduled to land at exit D-3, but owing to heavy fire it was shifted east to E-1, and the 18th Inf soon landed nearby.

G | BEACH GROUPS & LANDING CRAFT CREW

(Additional material by Martin Windrow)

Beach Group advance parties began landing on the British and Canadian beaches at H-Hour, followed by the remainder; their tasks were to organize men and equipment for crossing the beach, under the direction of an RN Beach Master with an RN Beach Commando. Local defense and labor were provided by dedicated infantry units, joined as soon as possible by a wide range of support and service detachments. The first Beach Group elements ashore, west to east, were:

Gold: "J", "Q" & "T" RN Beach Commandos; *King sector*, 2nd Bn Bedfordshire & Hertfordshire Regt (9th Beach Group); *Jig sector*, 6th Bn Royal Border Regt (10th Beach Group).

Juno: "L", "P" & "S" RN Beach Cdos; *Mike sector*, 8th Bn The King's Regt (7th Beach Group); *Nan sector*, 5th Bn R. Berkshire Regt (8th Beach Group). The RCN's "W" Beach Cdo did not land until D+1, when they took over from the mauled RN "P" Beach Cdo on Juno.

Sword: "F" & "R" RN Beach Cdos; 5th Bn The King's Regt (5th Beach Group).

1: Leading Seaman, "T" Royal Navy Beach Commando; Gold Beach

No longer under direct fire, he has discarded his Mk II helmet for a knit "cap, comforter." On Army battledress he wears all insignia on Navy-blue backing: on both sleeves the white "R.N. COMMANDO" title, and a red Combined Operations badge on a tombstone-shaped patch; on the left sleeve his red foul-anchor LS rating badge, and a 3-years' good conduct stripe, balanced on the right (obscured here) by his specialty badge – the crowned crossed flags of chief yeoman of signals. The *Beach Commando Monthly Memoranda* between May 1943 and January 1944 listed most of the unit lanyards, saying in May 1943 that they were worn on the right shoulder, but photos show them on the left: F = white, H = old gold, J = black, L = green; N (May '43) = red, but this later worn by R; P = light blue, Q = dark blue, R (from Sept '43) = red; S = maroon, T = gold/black twist; U = red/blue twist; V = violet.

Each Beach Cdo comprised three numbered parties (e.g. T1, T2 & T3) of three officers and 25 ratings. The party's weapons are listed as a stripped .303in Lewis LMG with tripod mount, three of these Lanchester 9mm M1928 SMGs, 10x .303in rifles, and 15x .455in revolvers; the web equipment was RN 1919 or standard 37 Ptn apart from the special pouches for the Lanchester's 50-round magazines. This sailor wears RN plimsolls, though "rope-soled shoes" are mentioned for beach work. (Source: www.relaysystem.co.uk/KSB BCMM)

2: Lance-corporal, 241 HQ Provost Company, Corps of Military Police, 5th Beach Group; Hermanville

Traffic control off and behind the beaches was a vital task, and CMP companies began landing with other Beach Group personnel from about H+30, operating on foot until their motorbikes arrived. His motorcyclist's helmet bears the MPs' ¾in red stripe below a narrower white Beach Group stripe, both broken at the front by a red "MP" on blue; the white stripe is also broken by a white rank chevron on the left side. His BD is worn with black three-buckle motorcyclist's boots. His sleeve insignia are the dark blue-on-red "C.M.P." title, above the red anchor on a red-edged white disc common to all Beach Group units, and his rank chevron. His 37 Ptn web equipment shows mismatched pouches – the Mk I on his right sits lower on the belt than the Mk II on his left. Photos of British MPs serving with 7th Beach Group on Juno show them additionally wearing the red-on-dark blue "MP" right-arm brassard that is absent here, and with the Beach Group disc superimposed on 3rd Cdn Div's patch, as in figure G4.

3: Landing craft coxswain, 528 LCA Flotilla, Royal Canadian Navy; HMCS *Prince Henry*, Juno Beach

The RCN's 528 Flotilla had seven landing craft, of which the LCAs with pennant numbers 850, 925, and 1021 were commanded by RCN Volunteer Reserve leading seamen, 1321 by an able seaman, 1033 by a sub-lieutenant, and 736 & 1372 by lieutenants. This leading seaman coxswain wears the badge of a leading stoker on the right sleeve of his blue jumper, and "CANADA" shoulder titles. His helmet is shrouded with the Army anti-gas cover, here with the neck-curtain cut off. His spray-scarf is a towel tucked into the neck of his Canadian-designed life vest; its "head-up" kapok-padded collar was awkward when a helmet was worn, and sailors often cut its supporting strings. Across the back of the shoulders the vest bore large white stenciling "R.C.N." above a serial number (e.g. "A6845," "A7583," "L5282," etc.), and sometimes the individual's name. (*Militaria Magazine* No. 277, August 2008)

4: Sergeant, 5th Bn Royal Berkshire Regt, 8th Beach Group; Juno Beach

This typical "badly wrapped parcel" is from a group photographed embarking on landing craft aboard HMCS *Prince Henry*. Oddly, all of them show the white Beach Group helmet-stripe recently painted out. The life belt is worn under web equipment, which incorporates double cartridge-carriers rather than basic pouches. The haversack attached at the left side shows the usual tea mug, and an air/ground recognition panel. A large bedroll made with a late-pattern groundsheet is strapped and tied around the "large pack" on his back, with a pair of brown plimsolls tied to it, and his rifle, with breech cover, balanced overall. He also has his respirator, rolled anti-gas cape, and a bandoleer slung around him as best he can with straps and tapes. He wears no regimental shoulder title; the insignia are the Beach Group disc superimposed on 3rd Cdn Div's patch, above what seems to be the Berkshires' traditional red "Brandywine" flash.

When their immediate task was completed Beach Group infantry battalions were not withdrawn; the 5th Berkshires stayed in the line in Normandy until August, being reduced to just 152 all ranks.

By early afternoon the crisis had passed, and the reinforced 1st Inf Div was solidly lodged. By evening, with 34,250 troops ashore, elements of the 116th and the Ranger Group had secured the western flank at Vierville. Battalions of the 8th, 16th, 115th, and 116th Inf were intermingled from exit D-3, extending east to just south of Colleville. The 1/16th and 2/18th effected the deepest penetrations south of Colleville, over 3,000yds inland. Casualties on Omaha were at least 700 dead, 330 missing, and 1,350 wounded, along with 50 tanks and 26 artillery pieces lost.

There were four Medal of Honor recipients on D-Day, three of them from the 1st Inf Div and one in the 4th: Pvt Carlton W. Barrett of C/1/18th Inf; 1st Lt Jimmie W. Monteith, Jr., of L/3/16th Inf; Tech 5 John J. Pinder, Jr., of HQ Co, 16th Inf (posthumous); and BrigGen Theodore D. Roosevelt, Jr., of HQ, 4th Inf Division.

Jut ashore and still wearing their life belts, soldiers perform urgent first aid on a casualty suffering from a back wound. Note the large size of the shingle; mainly accumulated in banks at the high-tide line, this was difficult for even tracked AFVs to cross. Later the shingle would mostly be removed by engineers and used for inland road beds. (Tom Laemlein/ Armor Plate Press)

GOLD

The British and Canadian beaches were comparatively narrower, with the main defenses directly on the seawalls, and the ground behind the beaches rising only 15–30 feet.

Gold was just under 6,000yds wide, comprising Jig Green and Red on the right (west) and King Green and Red on the left. Further right were Item Red and Green, which would be attacked from inland as elements from Jig Green swung westward, to secure that flank at Arromanches-les-Bains and contact the Americans on Omaha. There were six strongpoints on the Gold beaches and seven behind them. Half the beach area was edged by a low causeway and seawall running parallel to the shore, behind which Jig Red and King Green were backed by a flooded, boggy area 3,000yds long by 100–700yds wide. Beach obstacles were numerous and close to shore. Mines lined the seawall and surrounded strongpoints, and numerous AT guns positioned to enfilade the beaches (particularly at Le Hamel, Wn-37, and the Customs House, Wn-36) would extract a high price.

After 90 minutes' naval bombardment, the veteran 50th Inf Div's assault wave began landing at 07:30 hours. On Jig Green to the west, 231 Inf Bde were led ashore by 1st Hampshires and 1st Dorsets, to be followed by 2nd Devons at 08:15; King Red to the east was assigned to 69 Inf Bde (6th Green Howards and 5th East Yorks, followed at 08:20 by 7th Green Howards). The follow-on force would be 151 Inf Bde (6th, 7th, & 9th Durham Lt Inf), and the attached 56 Inf Bde (2nd South Wales Borderers, 2nd Glosters and 2nd Essex). Tanks were provided by 8 Armd Bde's Sherwood Rangers (to support 231 Inf Bde) and 4th/7th Royal Dragoon Guards (69 Inf Brigade), and there were three SP artillery regiments.

Sea conditions dictated that the amphibious Shermans had to be carried in much closer than planned, and some were landed late directly onto the beaches. Eight of the Sherwood Rangers' DDs were lost, and others became mingled with the LCTs carrying the specialist obstacle-clearing

Although the photo censors have obscured the number on the front of the superstructure and bow, this is LCI(L)-85, which took multiple hits on the starboard side from shore guns – note the mast hanging down into the water. Despite a heavy list this craft returned to port under its own power, and was repaired. (Tom Laemlein/Armor Plate Press)

Following 231 Bde ashore on Gold/Jig Green at about H+90, these marines of 47 RM Cdo had suffered many casualties on the run-in, losing four out of their 14 LCAs. They were also landed too far east, among these crowded LCTs unloading 231 Bde's priority vehicles. The corporal carrying a Thompson SMG is clearly wearing a battle jerkin; 47 was the only RM Cdo to be completely issued with these, in both full and "skeleton" versions.

British landing craft were usually painted very light blue, often with minimal irregular bands of mid-blue or black. The "pennant" numbers were allocated to flotillas randomly (see under Plate C3), and simply identified the individual craft – e.g., as here, "LC A431" and "LC T858," with the first two letters painted smaller. (IWM B5246)

AFVs from 79th Armd Division. Congestion forced LCAs to land wherever they could find space, and some craft were lost to mined obstacles. Pushed east by the current, 231 Bde came ashore to find that none of the defenses had been knocked out, and their expected tank and specialist AFV support was late or disorganized. The 1st Hampshires and 1st Dorsets received heavy fire and became pinned down, and many of the "flails" and AVREs were knocked out before they could clear paths. Communications broke down, making it almost impossible to call for naval and SP artillery support. Gunfire was especially heavy from Le Hamel (Wn-37) on the western flank.

The 5th East Yorks and 6th Green Howards of 69 Inf Bde landed on King Red, where fire was initially lighter until LCTs began landing Shermans of 4th/7th Royal Dragoon Guards onto the beach. This caused crowding at the waterline; guns in strongpoint Wn-33 at La Riviére to their east began knocking out the armor, and intense MG fire raked the infantry, pinning the 5th East Yorks at the seawall. It took all morning to clear La Rivière so that tanks and infantry could begin moving inland, clearing batteries and defensive positions as they went. The 6th Green Howards, backed up by their 7th Bn, made faster progress off the King beaches; with tank and AVRE support they knocked out bunkers, secured an exit, and took many prisoners.

From 11:00hrs, 56 and 151 Inf Bdes began landing; both encountered fire, but this was now less intense. Confusion and congestion slowed movement inland, however; Le Hamel held off repeated assaults, each strongpoint and fortified house falling only after stiff resistance, and it was not until 16:00hrs that the west flank had been cleared.

By the day's end the 50th Inf Div's brigades had penetrated an average of 5 miles. 69 Brigade were due south, having linked on their left with the Canadians from Juno; 151 Bde were on 69's right flank; 56 Bde were to the southwest approaching Bayeux, while 231 covered the west side of the beachhead and had secured Arromanches. 47 RM Commando were about 4 further miles west, but after suffering heavy casualties they had not been able to take their objective at Port-en-Bessin for a link-up with Omaha. Some 25,000 troops were landed on Gold; for many years an estimate of approximately 1,100 casualties, of which 350 dead, was accepted, but more recent research by the US National D-Day Memorial Foundation suggests a total of at least 2,000.

JUNO

The Canadians would land in the 6,500yd-wide Juno Area, which included Mike Green and Red beaches on the west and Nan Green, White, and Red to the east. These were dominated by four evacuated villages: from west to east, Graye-sur-Mer, Courseulles-sur-Mer, Bernières-sur-Mer, and St Aubin-sur-Mer. These had been fortified, and were protected by six beachside strongpoints and other scattered positions, so house-to-house fighting would be necessary. Obstacles were placed near the seawall; the Nan beaches had extensive rock reefs exposed at low tide, and numerous minefields made breakouts inland difficult.

The 3rd Cdn Inf Div's assault formations were: on Mike Green and Red beaches, 7 Inf Bde (Royal Winnipeg Rifles, Regina Rifle Regt, and 1st Bn Canadian Scottish as follow-up); and to their east on Nan White and Red, 8 Inf Bde (Queen's Own Rifles of Canada, North Shore (New Brunswick) Regt, and Régt de la Chaudière following up). From 2 Cdn Armd Bde, DDs from 6th Armd Regt (1st Hussars) would support 7 Bde and 10th Armd Regt (Fort Garry Horse) 8 Brigade. The reserve was 9 Inf Bde (Highland Lt Inf of Canada, Stormont, Dundas & Glengarry Highlanders, and North Nova Scotia Highlanders), plus 27th Armd Regt (Sherbrooke Fusiliers). Three regiments of SP artillery would also be landed among the support elements.

The Canadians planned to land at 07:45hrs, a little later than the British owing to the need for a higher tide to cover the reefs, but they still found themselves among obstacle belts. The leading elements of 7 Bde landed at 07:49 and 8 Bde's at 07:55, and as on other beaches the rough sea meant that DD tanks had to swim and wade ashore from much closer in than planned.

Film frame showing men of the North Shore (New Brunswick) Regt, 8 Cdn Inf Bde, disembarking under fire from an LCA on Juno/Nan Red opposite large seafront villas in St Aubin-sur-Mer. In the foreground, note a bangalore torpedo being carried; when British or Canadian pioneers (combat engineers within the HQ companies of infantry units) accompanied a rifle platoon in a landing craft they usually went down the ramp immediately following the platoon commander and his runner. At left is the LCA's port bow station, with a loopholed armor shield for a Lewis gun, and at right the coxswain. (IWM FLM 2569)

During street fighting, men of B Co, North Shore Regt, take cover in the Rue Canet, St Aubin-sur-Mer, at the remains of a roadblock of railway iron and heavy logs protecting strongpoint Wn-27; the barricade had eventually been destroyed by Petard projectiles from 79th Armd Div AVREs. This view looks north toward the beach; just visible at the far end is the roof of the concrete emplacement housing a 5cm gun. (IWM B5228)

This delayed them, and the British specialist armor was also landed late and out of place, denying the infantry much-needed support. The bombardments had made little impression on the defenses; the Canadians had to advance under heavy artillery, mortar, and machine-gun fire, and take pillboxes by their own resources. Many companies were initially pinned down, and suffered up to 50 percent losses. It took considerable time, effort, and cost in men and armor to get off the beaches, and particularly to clear the defended streets of Courseulles, which held up 7 Inf Bde until early afternoon.

H BRITISH LCA LOADS
(Additional material by Martin Windrow)

535 or 543 Flotilla, HMS *Glenearn*, carrying A Co, 1st Bn South Lancashire Regt to Sword/Queen White

Unlike the LCVP, the Landing Craft Assault had a steel hull, and partial overhead armor and armored doors inside the ramp gave some protection. It could not carry a vehicle or artillery piece owing to the fixed lengthways bench seats, and the narrow ramp made it slow to unload bulky items. Behind the armored doors on the left was a partly enclosed crew station for an LMG, and on the right another, with an overhead armor hatch, housing the coxswain's controls. The four-man RN (or very often, Royal Marines) crew were: a port bowman (forward davit hooks, doors, ramp, and the LMG); a coxswain (at the helm, starboard bow station) connected by a voice tube to a stoker/mechanic (stern, engine controls); and a sternsheetsman (stern davits, and signaling). One junior officer commanded every five LCAs, though RCN flotillas might have more officers.

The LCA's official capacity was 35 troops – two fewer than a platoon plus its habitual attachment (three sections of ten, plus platoon commander and his runner, platoon sergeant, two-man 2in mortar crew, plus two-man PIAT crew attached from company HQ). When embarking, the 1st Section took the seat closest to the ship's side, 2nd Sect the furthest, and 3rd Sect the central seat. On D-Day, the five A Co "serials" (NB, these identified the boat parties, *not* the LCAs' pennant numbers) for Queen/White had at most 33 men (serials 119 and 121), and serial 117 had only 30 plus four advance personnel from the Beach Group. Serials 118 and 120 consisted of personnel from A Co HQ and an attached Assault Demolition Team (see Plate F4), plus half-loads of stores. The excluded riflemen presumably joined the company's "left out of battle" replacement pool.

Serial 119
See color key, assuming this is a starboard-side craft from the landing ship. This is our *guess* at a plausible reduced platoon of 33: a rifleman from 3rd Sect serves as the officer's runner, and the rearmost rifleman of 1st Sect has been grabbed by the platoon sergeant to serve as ammunition carrier for the 2in mortar.

Number key, HQ & 3rd Section, from bow to stern: 1 = platoon commander; 2 = runner (from 3rd Sect); 3 = corporal sect cmdr; 4 & 5 = Bren Nos. 1 & 2; 6 = lance-cpl Bren group leader; 7–11 = riflemen. *HQ group:* 12 = mortar No. 2 (from 1st Sect); 13 = mtr No. 1; 14 & 15 = PIAT Nos. 1 & 2, from A Co HQ; 16 = platoon sergeant.

Serial 118
This carried a half-load of stores and spare equipment, plus 14 men from A Co HQ.

Key: 1 = company cmdr; 2 & 3 = runners; 4 & 5 = signalers w. No. 18 set; 6–10 = pioneers w. bangalores; 11 & 12 = litter- (stretcher-) bearers; 13 = intel NCO; 14 = regimental police NCO.

Serial 120
This also carried stores, plus ten men from A Co HQ, and a five-man ADT from 246 Fld Co RE.

Key: 1 = CSM; 2 = runner; 3 = sniper; 4 = signaler w. No. 46 set; 5 & 6 = sigs w. No. 18 set; 7–10 = litter-bearers. *Plus:* 11 = ADT NCO; 12 & 13 = 75lb charge; 14 = 40lb charge; 15 = flamethrower. (Source: http://ww2talk.com/forums/topic/38764-sword-beach)

Assault units were divided between different landing ships – e.g., at Sword/Queen White, A & C Cos of the 1st South Lancs were aboard the LSI(L) *Glenearn;* the follow-up D Co and battalion HQ were on *Empire Battleaxe*, and the follow-up B Co on *Empire Cutlass* (which had already launched the first-wave A & B Cos, 2nd East Yorks for Queen Red).

LCA flotilla strengths varied; e.g., RM 535 & 543 Flotillas allocated to *Glenearn* had respectively ten and 11 (two of the latter being assigned to special duties). For the "first flight" at 06:00hrs, six craft were lowered on both port and starboard sides, and for the "second flight" at 06:30, four each side. Only one of these LCAs was lost in action, but many flotillas suffered much worse; for instance, collectively the landing ships *Prince Henry, Prince David, Princess Astrid, Princess Charlotte* and *Victoria* lost 29 out of their 38 LCAs.

Serial 119

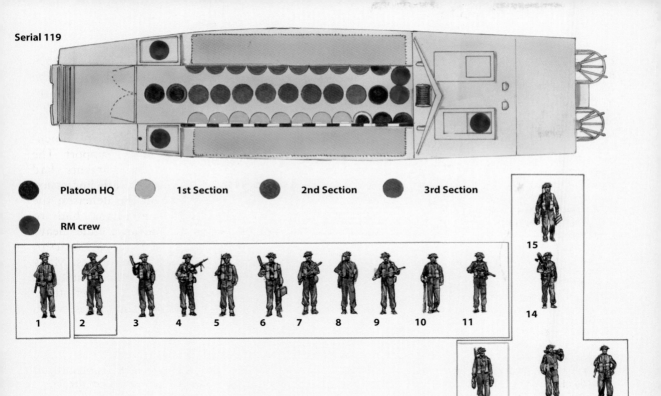

Platoon HQ   1st Section   2nd Section   3rd Section

RM crew

1 2 3 4 5 6 7 8 9 10 11

15 14

12 13 16

Serial 118

1 2 4 8 10 12 13

3 5 6 7 9 11 14

Serial 120

2 5 9 12 14

1 3 4 6 7 8 10 11 13 15

One man in this LCA from the landing ship *Llangby Castle* off Juno displays the white-on-black shoulder title "ROYAL WINNIPEG RIFLES/ CANADA;" the Winnipegs were the assault battalion on Mike Red beach, but this photo was clearly taken later in the day. At least two of the boats are also riding too high to be fully loaded, when they had a draft of only 1ft 9in forward and 2ft 3in aft. Despite having twin engines, the steel LCA was considered underpowered, with a loaded speed of only 6 knots – about half that of the wooden American LCVP.

D-Day was far from over for an LCA crew once they had landed their first assault "serial;" they would return to their ships to embark follow-up infantry or support troops, and later ferried wounded or prisoners out for shipment back to England.

On D-Day landing ships and craft were not confined to carrying troops of their own nations; e.g., the Royal Navy's 551 Flotilla LCAs landed the GIs of Co A, 1/116th Infantry on Omaha/Dog Green, and 552 Flotilla from the *Empire Gauntlet* carried troops of 1/8th Infantry to Utah. The Royal Marine 535 Flotilla from the *Empire Broadsword* landed first-wave British assault troops on Sword before ferrying US follow-up troops to Utah. (L & A Canada PA-132651, photographer unidentified)

Once the gun tanks, flails, and AVREs arrived, exits were gradually secured and the Canadians moved south into open country, clearing numerous villages and pushing deep, with the support of the reserve 9 Bde after this had finally escaped the massive coastal traffic-jams. On their east flank, 48 RM Cdo landed at 08:45, and moved to link up with the British on Sword, but this was not accomplished; they had taken 50 percent casualties by the time they reached their first objective at Langrune-sur-Mer. At the day's end Juno and Sword were still separated by a 2-mile gap, which served as a corridor for 21. Panzer-Div elements to launch a counterattack on 3rd Brit Inf Div – though this came to nothing, and at high cost.

While none of the Allied assault divisions reached their D-Day objective lines, the Canadians made the most relative progress. They had hoped to reach the outskirts of Caen, but got no further than the near edge of Carpiquet airfield just over a mile west of it. The Queen's Own Rifles was the only unit to actually secure its day's objective, the small village of Anisy. Juno was the second most costly beach after Omaha: of the 21,400 troops landed on June 6, the casualties were recorded as 340 Canadian dead, 574 wounded, and 47 captured, but recent research has increased the estimated total to more than 1,200.

SWORD

At Sword, almost the entire frontage of Queen and the flanking Peter and Roger sectors was lined by the buildings of villages straggling eastwards and swelling into Ouistreham, a small harbor town at the mouth of the Orne River and Caen Canal. There were three lines of near-shore obstacles, and four beachside strongpoints: from west to east "Trout" (Wn-21) in Lion-sur-Mer, "Cod" (Wn-20) at La Bréche, and "the Casino" and "Riva Bella-Ouistreham" (Wn-18). Of these "Cod" was the most threatening, sitting astride the junction of Queen Red and White. Boggy ground behind the villages would hamper AFVs, and four more substantial strongpoints were situated inland. Across the parallel Orne River and canal to the southeast, the British 6th Abn Div had glidered and parachuted in advance

Planned unit landing sequence, reinforced 3rd (Brit) Inf Div, Sword/Queen White & Red

This is also representative of the type of reinforcements to 50th Inf Div on Gold. As there, sea conditions, losses, and delays offshore disrupted parts of the plan. Attachments and advance parties from many support and service units, also present, are not listed here.

H-Hour to H+120 (07:30–09:30hrs):

(1)   A & B Sqns, 13th/18th Royal Hussars, 27 Armd Bde – 40x Sherman DD tanks. Breaching Teams & Obstacle Clearance Teams, 5 Assault Regt RE, 79th Armd Div – specialized AFVs. 5th (RM) Armd Support Bty – 16x Centaur tanks.

(2)   8 Inf Bde assault infantry – A & C Cos, 1st Bn South Lancs; A & B Cos, 2nd Bn East Yorks.

(3)   Detachments, 629 Field Sqn RE – obstacle demolitions; & 246 Field Co RE – mine clearance & assault demolition teams.

(4)   33rd & 76th Field Regts RA – 48x SP 105mm guns.

(5)   Follow-up infantry companies – B & D Cos, 1st S. Lancs; C & D Cos, 2nd E. Yorks; both Bn HQs.

(6)   Beach Groups – RN Beach Cdos; inf 5th Bn King's Regt; misc services 4 Commando & 41 RM Cdo (flank operations).

(7)   8 Inf Bde vehicles, plus further specialized AFVs.

(8)   1st Bn Suffolk Regt (8 Inf Bde reserve).

(9)   1 Special Service Bde follow-up elements.

(10)   8th Inf Bde vehicles & stores. 7th Field Regt RA – 24x 105mm SP guns.

H+150 to H+250 (10:00–11:40hrs):

(11)   185 Inf Bde (intermediate bde): 2nd Bn King's Shropshire Lt Inf.

(12)   Staffordshire Yeomanry, 27 Armd Bde – DD Sherman tanks.

(13)   2nd Bn Royal Warwickshire Regt.

(14)   1st Bn Royal Norfolk Regt.

(15)   185 Inf Bde vehicles & stores.

(16)   9 Inf Bde (reserve bde): 2nd Bn Lincolnshire Regt.

(17)   1st Bn King's Own Scottish Borderers.

(18)   2nd Bn Royal Ulster Rifles.

(19)   1st East Riding Yeomanry, 27 Armd Bde – Sherman tanks.

(20)   9 Inf Bde vehicles & stores.

(For greater detail see: http://ww2talk.com/forums/topic/38764-sword-beach)

Looking inland on Sword/ Queen Red: troops sheltering beside a Churchill AVRE of 79 Asslt Sqn, 5 Asslt Regt RE from 79th Armd Division. Scheduled to land at H-Hour, the four troop-strength Breaching Teams on Sword were each tasked to clear a 225yd-wide lane to one of the beach exits. Each team had one AVRE bridge-layer, one with frame-mounted bangalore ("Boase") torpedoes and a log "carpet," one with bangalores and "Bobbin" matting, and two flail tanks. (IWM B5096)

elements to secure the Benouville bridges and Merville battery and thus Sword's eastern flank. After linking up with the Airborne, the reinforced British 3rd Inf Div's main D-Day objective was to reach the outskirts of Caen.

Sherman DD tank of B Sqn, 13th/18th Hussars with its screen folded down, in action in support of 4 Cdo in Ouistreham, apparently on the lateral east–west road running behind Sword Beach; most of the commandos wear battle jerkins. This unit's advance inland had been delayed by the prolonged resistance of strongpoint "Cod," and by the arrival of the DD tanks about 90 minutes late. (IWM MH2011)

German prisoners stand in the sea beside one of many "funnies" disabled during the initial landings in the Sword/Queen sector. This is a wading Sherman Crab anti-mine flail tank of 22nd Dragoons, from either one of the Breaching Teams (see caption opposite) or Obstacle Clearance Teams of 5 Asslt Regt Royal Engineers. Landed from H-Hour simultaneously with the Breaching Teams and sometimes mixed with them in the same LCT loads, the four Obstacle Clearance Teams each had four Sherman flails and four Churchill AVREs, the latter with "Bullshorn" mine-plows and all with drag chains and hooks, plus D7 bulldozers from 860 Mechanical Equipment Section RE, and towed armored sledges. (IWM B5089).

Unlike on Gold and Juno, where two assault brigades landed abreast, 3rd Inf Div opted to run ashore in a single column of three brigades and support units arrayed in a number of successive echelons (panel on page 57). The spearhead would be 8 Inf Bde (2nd Bn East Yorkshire Regt, 1st Bn South

Evening, June 6: gunners of either 76 or 33 Field Regt RA, 3rd Div – note the deep-wading trunking still in place on the self-propelled 105mm Priest – watch some of the gliders flying 6 Air-Landing Bde toward the complex of landing zones around Ranville. (IWM B5046)

Evening, June 6: after the link-up between 1 Special Service Bde and 6th Abn Div on the eastern flank of the British beachhead, commandos dig in at LZ "N" between Ranville and Sallenelles, with abandoned Horsa gliders in the background. (IWM B5051)

Lancashire Regt, followed by 1st Bn Suffolk Regiment). The intermediate force was 185 Inf Bde (2nd Bn King's Shropshire Lt Inf, 2nd Bn Royal Warwickshire Regt, 1st Bn Royal Norfolk Regt), and the reserve 9 Inf Bde (2nd Bn Lincolnshire Regt, 1st Bn King's Own Scottish Borderers, 2nd Bn Royal Ulster Rifles). The division was supported by 27 Armd Bde (13th/18th Royal Hussars and Staffordshire Yeomanry partly equipped with DDs, and 1st East Riding Yeomanry), and three regiments of SP artillery.

The LCAs carrying 8 Inf Bde began their run to shore at 06:00 to land on the 1,500yd-wide Queen Red and White. The DD tanks were launched 5,000yds out, and three of the 34 sank. The bombardments had done little damage, and German strongpoints opened a heavy fire as the LCAs approached. Beach obstacles also took a toll; formation began to degrade, with troops from different companies sometimes landing muddled together.

At 07:25 the lead infantry wave landed, mixed up with DD tanks and specialist armor. Engineers had difficulties in clearing obstacles, and the tideline became congested with landing craft. Many of the assault troops were cut down as they debarked, since it was 2½ hours before the main strongpoint, "Cod," was finally overrun. 4 Commando and 41 RM Cdo were landed next. 4 Commando on the left successfully captured the Casino strongpoint and Ouistreham, clearing the way for 1 Special Service Bde to march inland and link with the Airborne around Benouville at 13:10 hours. On the right, however, 41 RM Cdo, tasked with taking strongpoint "Trout" at Lion-sur-Mer, met such strong resistance that the unit was unable to move any further west to link up with Juno.

Led off the beach by the specialist AFVs from 79th Armd Div, units began working their way inland from 08:30 hours. Despite stubborn resistance at strongpoint "Cod," elements of all three 8 Inf Bde units pushed south to engage the inland strongpoints "Sole," "Daimler," "Morris," and "Hillman," backed by units of the intermediate 185 Inf Bde landed from 10:00hrs with additional armor. From 13:00 the reserve 9 Inf Bde began landing; when it extricated itself from the congestion it was sent to consolidate the left flank, held by the lightly equipped Airborne and Commando units. At 15:00hrs the advance toward Caen, led by 185 Inf Bde's 2nd KSLI with some Staffordshire Yeomanry tanks, ran out of steam when it was hit by the first of 21. Panzer-Div's counterattacks in the gap between Sword and Juno.

The end of D-Day found 185 Inf Bde with the furthest southern penetration, 3 miles short of Caen. 9 Infantry Brigade was defending the southwestern flank, inland from 8 Inf Bde; and the southeast, across the Orne and the canal, was now held by the newly landed remainder of 6th Abn Division. The British had landed 28,845 troops on Sword, while suffering 683 casualties, of whom about one-third were killed – fewer than expected.

COST & AFTERMATH

Sources still conflict over the numbers of casualties on each beach. These, especially the dead and missing, were sometimes not reported for days. Wounded were evacuated more or less randomly to different ships for treatment and evacuation, and some were not reported to their units until after they were hospitalized in England. Ongoing research by the US National D-Day Memorial Foundation has significantly increased earlier estimates, particularly for Omaha, and suggests total D-Day casualties for the Allied armies of around 7,800 (perhaps 4,275 US, 2,327 British, and 1,204 Canadian), of whom 2,499 Americans and 1,915 British and Canadians were killed. No final figure is ever likely to be reached.

Only two of the beaches – Juno and Gold – were linked on the first day. Omaha and Utah linked up only on June 10, and all five beachheads were not connected until June 12. Progress inland was slow from all five beaches, as units overcame resolute defenses and fought off counterattacks by German

Beyond a scatter of discarded kit, British dead lie covered with their groundsheets in front of strongpoint "Cod" on the Sword/Queen beaches. This position did not finally fall – after attacks by men from 1st South Lancs, 2nd East Yorks, 4 Cdo and 5th Beach Group, supported by flail and gun tanks – until about 10:00hrs/ H+150. (IWM B5118)

Medics rigging a plasma transfusion bottle to treat one of their own – one of at least 1,350 US wounded on Omaha. Medics did not yet display red crosses on helmets, but these soon came into widespread use. (NARA)

reinforcements. For four days from June 19 the beachhead was disrupted by the worst storm to hit Normandy in 40 years; one of the two prefabricated Mulberry Harbors was destroyed and the other badly damaged, greatly hampering the delivery of reinforcements and supplies. The Americans seized the critical port of Cherbourg on June 25, and finally broke out at St Lô on July 25; meanwhile the vicious battle for Caen, which attracted the bulk of the German armored reinforcements, occupied the British and Canadians for two months until it finally fell on August 6. The overall Battle of Normandy raged on until August 25, at a cost of over 226,000 Allied and at least 500,000 German casualties.

SELECT BIBLIOGRAPHY

Beevor, Antony, *D-Day: The Battle for Normandy* (Penguin Group, 2009)
Bernage, Georges, *Gold, Juno, Sword* (Editions Heimdal, 2003)
Bertin, François, *Allied Liberation Vehicles, 1944* (Casemate, 2007)
Bertin, François, *D-Day Normandy: Weapons, Uniforms, Military Equipment* (Casemate, 2007)
Bouchery, Jean, *The British Soldier: From D-Day to VE-Day, Vols 1 & 2* (Histoire & Collections, 1998 & 1999)

Bouchery, Jean, *The Canadian Soldier: From D-Day to VE-Day – Organization, Uniforms, Insignia, Equipment, Armament, Tanks and Vehicles* (Histoire & Collections, 2003)

Bowden, Mark & Ambrose, Stephen, *Our Finest Day: June 6, 1944* (Chronicle Books, 2002)

Ford, Ken, *D-Day 1944 (3): Sword Beach & the British Airborne Landings*, Campaign 105 (Osprey, 2002)

Ford, Ken, *D-Day 1944 (4): Gold & Juno Beaches*, Campaign 112 (Osprey, 2002)

Fowler, Will, *D-Day: The First 24 Hours* (Lewis International, 2003)

Gawne, Jonathan, *Spearheading D-Day: American Special Units in Normandy* (Histoire & Collections, 1998)

Gawne, Jonathan, *Lessons Learned in Combat: D-Day and Beyond* (Bellacourage Books, 2013)

Hall, Tony (ed.), *D-Day: The Strategy, The Men, The Equipment* (MBI Publishing, 2001)

Holborn, Andrew, *56th Infantry Brigade and D-Day: An Independent Infantry Brigade and the Campaign in North West Europe 1944–1945* (Continuum, 2010)

Kershaw, Alex, *The Bedford Boys: One American Town's Ultimate Sacrifice* (Da Capo, 2003)

McManus, John C., *The Dead and Those About to Die. D-Day: The Big Red One at Omaha Beach* (Penguin Group, 2014)

Messenger, Charles, *The D-Day Atlas: Anatomy of the Normandy Campaign* (Thames & Hudson, 2014)

Milner, Marc, *Stopping the Panzers: The Untold Story of D-Day* (University Press of Kansas, 2016)

Morgan, Mike, *D-Day Hero: CSM Stanley Hollis VC* (Sutton Publishing, 2004)

Naval Institute Press, *Allied Landing Craft of World War Two* (Naval Institute Press, 1985)

Reynolds, Michael, *Eagles & Bulldogs in Normandy 1944: The American 29th Division from Omaha to St Lo & The British 3rd Division from Sword to Caen* (Casemate, 2003)

Ross, John, *The Forecast for D-Day and the Weatherman Behind Ike's Greatest Gamble* (Lyons Press / Globe Pequot Press, 2014)

Sadler, Ian, "The British 1942 Battle Jerkin (1)," in *Military Illustrated Past & Present* No. 27 (August 1990)

Stewart, Andrew, *Caen Controversy: The Battle for Sword Beach 1944* (Helion, 2014)

Zaloga, Steven J., *D-Day 1944 (1): Omaha Beach*, Campaign 100 (Osprey, 2003)

Zaloga, Steven J., *D-Day 1944 (2): Utah Beach & the US Airborne Landings*, Campaign 104 (Osprey, 2004)

Zuehlke, Mark, *Juno Beach: Canada's D-Day Victory – June 6, 1944* (Douglas & McIntyre, 2009)

INDEX

Figures in **bold** refer to illustrations.

artillery
105mm Priests **59**
bangalores 31, **31**, 53
British overview 24–25
concrete emplacements **10**
mortar round tubes **4**, 19, **F1** (41)
mortars 35
organization 29, 34
US overview 17
Assault Demolition Teams 36, **F4** (41)

beach groups **G** (49)
beach obstacles 8–10, **9**
clearance **D** (27), 37, **F4** (41), 42, 58
beaches 5–8, **5**
exiting 9–10
boat teams 30–32, **E** (33), 36–37
British forces
in action 42, 43, 51–61, **52**
commandos 24, 34–36, **36**, **G1** (49), **52**,
56, 58, 60
organization 11, 32–37
training 10–12
uniforms and equipment 22–29, **28**, **F** (41)

Caen 56, 58, 61, 62
Canadian forces
in action 38, 53–56, **53**, **54**, **56**
landing craft crew **G3** (49)
organization 11, 32–37
training 10–12, **12**
uniforms and equipment 22–29, **23**
"Cod" strongpoint 57, 60, **61**
Courseulles-sur-Mer 53, 54

D-Day
landings 39–61
location and date 4–5, 37
number of troops landed 4
run-in 37–38
demolitions **D** (27), 37, **F4** (41)

equipment
ammo storage **4**, **A4–5** (7), **14**, **B** (15), 17,
18, **23**, 25, 26–28
assault jackets 19–22, **20**, 31
battle jerkins **25**, 28–29, **28**, **F** (41), **52**
bedrolls **A1–2** (15), 17, **28**, **F2** (41),
G4 (49)
binoculars **B8** (15), 19
British and Canadian overview 25–29, **25**
commandos 26, **28**, **36**, **52**
compasses **B7** (15), 19
dispatch (map) cases **B2** (15), **18**, 19, 28
entrenching and digging tools **A1–2** (7),
17, 25, 26
field bags ("musettes") **B2** (15), 17
first aid pouches **A1–2** (7), **B** (15), **18**,
19, 28
foxhole starter charges 19
gasmasks **4**, **A1–3** (7), **B1** (15), 16, 18, 19,
C5 (21), 23, 25
Hagensen packs **D5** (27)

haversacks and rucksacks **A** (7), **B1** (15),
17, 24, 25, 26, **G4** (49)
landing craft crew **C** (21)
life belts and vests **4**, **A11** (7), **B1** (15),
18, **C3–4** (21), 23, 39, **F2** (41), **G3–4**
(49), 50
military police **G2** (49)
for personal use 19, 25, 28
phrase books **B4–5** (15)
pyrotechnic projectors **B10** (15), **C6** (21)
US overview 17–22
water canteens and bottles **A1–2** (7), **B2**
(15), 17, **18**, 25
web gear **A1–2** (7), **B2** (15), 17, **23**, 25

food and rations **A9–10** (7), 17, 25
"frogmen" 37

Gap Assault Teams **D** (27), 37
gliders 60
Gold Beach 6, 48, 51–53, 61

Le Hamel 52
helmets and headgear
British and Canadian **23**, **23**, 28, **F** (41)
commandos 24, **36**, **G1** (49)
Gap Assault Teams **D1** (27)
landing craft crew **C** (21), **G3** (49)
military police **G2** (49)
US **4**, **A1–2** (7), 16, **32**
Hollis, Company Sergeant-Major Stanley
F3 (41)

insignia
British and Canadian **23**, **23**, 24, 38, **F**
(41), **G** (49)
military police **G2** (49)
US **14**, **B** (15), 16, **16**
Inverary Training Centre 10–12

Juno Beach 6, 48, 53–56, 61

landing
in practise **32**, **E** (33), 39–61
in theory 30–32, 36–37
landing craft
boarding 37
Canadian overview 48
crew **C** (21), **G3** (49), 54
crew's work on D-Day 56
LCAs **12**, 31, 38, 53, **H** (55), 56
LCI(L)s 43, 51
LCI(S)s **43**, 47
LCTs 34, 52
LCVPs **13**, 20, **32**, **E** (33), 46
loads **H** (55)
travelling in 37–38, **38**

medics 62
military police 35, **G2** (49)
mines 8, 9–10, **D6** (27)

Omaha Beach
fight for 45–50, **46**, **47**, **50**, 61, 62
terrain and geography 5, 6, 10

organization 11, 29–37
Ouistreham 57, **58**, 60

Pointe-du-Hoc 46–47

radios **B9** (15), 31–32, **45**

St Aubin-sur-Mer 53, **54**
seasickness 37–38
Sword Beach
beach groups 48
fight for **28**, 36, 42, 57–61, **58**, **59**, **61**
location 6

troop preparation and training 10–13,
12, **13**
"Trout" strongpoint 57, 60

uniforms
beach groups **G** (49)
British and Canadian 22–23, **23**, 28, 38,
F (41)
commandos 24, 36, **G1** (49)
Gap Assault Teams **D** (27), 37
landing craft crew **C** (21), **G3** (49)
US **A1–2** (7), 13–17, **14**, **B1–2** (15), **18**, 19
US forces
in action 43–50, **45**, **47**, **50**
Army Rangers 30, **31**
boat teams 30–32, **E** (33)
Coast Guardsmen 38
landing craft crew **C** (21)
organization 29–32
training 12–13, **13**
uniforms and equipment **4**, **A** (7), 13–22,
14, **B** (15), **18**, 19
Utah Beach 6, 43–45, 61

vehicles
amphibian trucks **D8** (27)
amphibious tanks **44**, **47**, 58
AVREs 35, 58
flail tanks 59
tank-dozers **D3** (27)
Universal Carriers 35

weapons
BARs **B1** (15)
bayonets **4**, **A1–2** (7), 17
beach groups **G1** (49)
British and Canadian overview 24–25
carbines **B2** (15), 16, **16**, 18, 24,
D1–2 (27)
commandos 24
flamethrowers **F4** (41)
grenades **4**, **A6–8** (7), **14**, **B6** (15), 17, 24
knives **14**, 17, **C7–8** (21)
LMGs 24
pistols **B2** (15), 18, 24
revolvers 24
rifles **4**, **A1–2** (7), **9**, **14**, 18, **23**, 24, 31
SMGs 16–17, 24, **F** (41), **52**
US overview 16–17
Woolacombe Assault Training Center 12–13